The True Story of Christopher Columbus
By Elbridge Brooks

PREFACE.

This "True Story of Christopher Columbus" is offered and inscribed to the boys and girls of America as the opening volume in a series especially designed for their reading, and to be called "Children's Lives of Great Men." In this series the place of honor, or rather of position, is given to Columbus the Admiral, because had it not been for him and for his pluck and faith and perseverance there might have been no young Americans, such as we know to-day, to read or care about the world's great men.

Columbus led the American advance; he discovered the New World; he left a record of persistence in spite of discouragement and of triumph over all obstacles, that has been the inspiration and guide for Americans ever since his day, and that has led them to work on in faith and hope until the end they strove for was won.

"The True Story of Christopher Columbus" will be followed by the "true story" of others who have left names for us to honor and revere, who have made the world better because they lived, and who have helped to make and to develop American freedom, strength and progress.

It will be the endeavor to have all these presented in the simple, straightforward, earnest way that appeals to children, and shows how the hero can be the man, and the man the hero. E. S. B.

THE TRUE STORY OF CHRISTOPHER COLUMBUS

CHAPTER I. BOY WITH AN IDEA.

Men who do great things are men we all like to read about. This is the story of Christopher Columbus, the man who discovered America. He lived four hundred years ago. When he was a little boy he lived in Genoa. It was a beautiful city in the northwestern part of the country called Italy. The mountains were behind it; the sea was in front of it, and it was so beautiful a place that the people who lived there called it "Genoa the Superb." Christopher Columbus was born in this beautiful city of Genoa in the year 1446, at number 27 Ponticello Street. He was a bright little fellow with a fresh-looking face, a clear eye and golden hair. His father's name was Domenico Columbus; his mother's name was Susanna. His father was a wool-comber. He cleaned and straightened out the snarled-up wool that was cut from the sheep so as to make it ready to be woven into cloth.

Christopher helped his father do this when he grew strong enough, but he went to school, too, and learned to read and write and to draw maps and charts. These charts were maps of the sea, to show the sailors where they could steer without running on the rocks and sand, and how to sail safely from one country to another.

This world was not as big then as it is now—or, should say, people did not know it was as big. Most of the lands that Columbus had studied about in school, and most of the people he had heard about, were in Europe and parts of Asia and Africa. The city of Genoa where Columbus lived was a very busy and a very rich city. It was on the Mediterranean Sea, and many of the people who lived there were sailors who went in their ships on voyages to distant lands. They sailed to other places on the Mediterranean Sea, which is a very large body of water, you know, and to England, to France, to Norway, and even as far away as the cold northern island of Iceland. This was thought to be a great journey.

The time in which Columbus lived was not as nice a time as is this in which you live. People were always quarreling and fighting about one thing or another, and the sailors who belonged to one country would try to catch and steal the ships or the things that belonged to the sailors or the storekeepers of another country. This is what we call piracy, and a pirate, you know, is thought to be a very wicked man.

But when Columbus lived, men did not think it was so very wicked to be a sort of half-way pirate, although they did know that they would be killed if they were caught. So almost every sailor was about half pirate. Every boy who lived near the seashore and saw the ships and the sailors, felt as though he would like to sail away to far-off lands and see all the strange sights and do all the brave things that the sailors told about. Many of them even said they would like to be pirates and fight with other sailors, and show how strong and brave and plucky they could be. Columbus was one of these. He was what is called an adventurous boy. He did not like to stay quietly at home with his father and comb out the tangled wool. He thought it would be much nicer to sail away to sea and be a brave captain or a rich merchant.

When he was about fourteen years old he really did go to sea. There was a captain of a sailing vessel that sometimes came to Genoa who had the same last name—Columbus. He was no relation, but the little Christopher somehow got acquainted with him among the wharves of Genoa. Perhaps he had run on errands for him, or helped him with some of the sea-charts he knew so well how to draw. At any rate he sailed away with this Captain Columbus as his cabin boy, and went to the wars with him and had quite an exciting life for a boy.

Sailors are very fond of telling big stories about their own adventures or about far-off lands and countries. Columbus, listened to many of these sea-stories, and heard many wonderful things about a very rich land away to the East that folks called Cathay.

If you look in your geographies you will not find any such place on the map as Cathay, but you will find China, and that was what men in the time of Columbus called Cathay. They told very big stories about this far-off Eastern land. They said its kings lived in golden houses, that they were covered with pearls and diamonds, and that everybody there was so rich that money was as plentiful as the stones in the street.

This, of course, made the sailors and storekeepers, who were part pirate, very anxious to go to Cathay and get some of the gold and jewels and spices and splendor for themselves. But Cathay was miles and miles away from Italy and Spain and France and England. It was away across the deserts and mountains and seas and rivers, and they had to give it up because they could not sail there.

At last a man whose name was Marco Polo, and who was a very brave and famous traveler, really did go there, in spite of all the trouble it took. And when he got back his stories were so very surprising that men were all the more anxious to find a way to sail in their ships to Cathay and see it for themselves.

But of course they could not sail over the deserts and mountains, and they were very much troubled because they had to give up the idea, until the son of the king of Portugal, named Prince Henry, said he believed that ships could sail around Africa and so get to India or "the Indies" as they called that land, and finally to Cathay.

Just look at your map again and see what a long, long voyage it would be to sail from Spain and around Africa to India, China and Japan. It is such a long sail that, as you know, the Suez Canal was dug some twenty years ago so that ships could sail through the Mediterranean Sea and out into the Indian Ocean, and not have to go away around Africa.

But when Columbus was a boy it was even worse than now, for no one really knew how long Africa was, or whether ships really could sail around it. But Prince Henry said he knew they could, and he sent out ships to try. He died before his Portuguese sailors, Bartholomew Diaz, in 1493, and Vasco de Gama, in 1497, at last did sail around it and got as far as "the Indies."

So while Prince Henry was trying to see whether ships could sail around Africa and reach Cathay in that way, the boy Columbus was listening to the stories the sailors told and was wondering whether some other and easier way to Cathay might not be found.

When he was at school he had studied about a certain man named Pythagoras, who had lived in Greece thousands of years before he was born, and who had said that the earth was round "like a ball or an orange."

As Columbus grew older and made maps and studied the sea, and read books and listened to what other people said, he began to believe that this man named Pythagoras might be right, and that the earth was round, though everybody declared it was flat. If it is round, he said to himself, "what is the use of trying to sail around Africa to get to Cathay? Why not just sail west from Italy or Spain and keep going right around the world until you strike Cathay? I believe it could be done," said Columbus.

By this time Columbus was a man. He was thirty years old and was a great sailor. He had been captain of a number of vessels; he had sailed north and south and east; he knew all about a ship and all about the sea. But, though he was so good a sailor, when he said that he believed the earth was round, everybody laughed at him and said that he was crazy. "Why, how can the earth be round?" they cried. "The water would all spill out if it were, and the men who live on the other side would all be standing on their heads with their feet waving in the air." And then they laughed all the harder.

But Columbus did not think it was anything to laugh at. He believed it so strongly, and felt so sure that he was right, that he set to work to find some king or prince or great lord to let him have ships and sailors and money enough to try to find a way to Cathay by sailing out into the West and across the Atlantic Ocean.

Now this Atlantic Ocean, the western waves of which break upon our rocks and beaches, was thought in Columbus's day to be a dreadful place. People called it the Sea of Darkness, because they did not know what was on the other side of it, or what dangers lay beyond that distant blue rim where the sky and water seem to meet, and which we call the horizon. They thought the ocean stretched to the end of a flat world, straight away to a sort of "jumping-off place," and that in this horrible jumping-off place were giants and goblins and dragons and monsters and all sorts of terrible things that would catch the ships and destroy them and the sailors.

So when Columbus said that he wanted to sail away toward this dreadful jumping-off place, the people said that he was worse than crazy. They said he was a wicked man and ought to be punished.

But they could not frighten Columbus. He kept on trying. He went from place to place trying to get the ships and sailors he wanted and was bound to have. As you will see in the next chapter, he tried to get help wherever he thought it could be had. He asked the people of his own home, the city of Genoa, where he had lived and played when a boy; he asked the people of the beautiful city that is built in the sea—Venice; he tried the king of Portugal, the king of England, the king of France the king and queen of Spain. But for a long time nobody cared to listen to such a wild and foolish and dangerous plan—to go to Cathay by the way of the Sea of Darkness and the Jumping-off place. You would never get there alive, they said.

And so Columbus waited. And his hair grew white while he waited, though he was not yet an old man. He had thought and worked and hoped so much that he began to look like an old man when he was forty years old. But still he would never say that perhaps he was wrong, after all. He said he knew he was right, and that some day he should find the Indies and sail to Cathay.

CHAPTER II. WHAT PEOPLE THOUGHT OF THE IDEA.

I do not wish you to think that Columbus was the first man to say that the earth was round, or the first to sail to the West over the Atlantic Ocean. He was not. Other men had said that they believed the earth was round; other men had sailed out into the Atlantic Ocean. But no sailor who believed the earth was round had ever yet tried to prove that it was by crossing the Atlantic. So, you see, Columbus was really the first man to say, I believe the earth is round and I will show you that it is by sailing to the lands that are on the other side of the earth.
He even figured out how far it was around the world. Your geography, you know, tells you now that what is called the circumference of the earth—that is, a straight line drawn right around it— is nearly twenty-five thousand miles. Columbus had figured it up pretty carefully and he thought it was about twenty thousand miles. If I could start from Genoa, he said, and walk straight ahead until I got back to Genoa again, I should walk about twenty thousand miles. Cathay, he thought, would take up so much land on the other side of the world that, if he went west instead of east, he would only need to sail about twenty-five hundred or three thousand miles.
If you have studied your geography carefully you will see what a mistake he made.
It is really about twelve thousand miles from Spain to China (or Cathay as he called it). But America is just about three thousand miles from Spain, and if you read all this story you will see how Columbus's mistake really helped him to discover America.
I have told you that Columbus had a longing to do something great from the time when, as a little boy, he had hung around the wharves in Genoa and looked at the ships sailing east and west and talked with the sailors and wished that he could go to sea. Perhaps what he had learned at school—how some men said that the earth was round—and what he had heard on the wharves about the wonders of Cathay set him to thinking and to dreaming that it might be possible for a ship to sail around the world without falling off. At any rate, he kept on thinking and dreaming and longing until, at last, he began doing.
Some of the sailors sent out by Prince Henry of Portugal, of whom I have told you, in their trying to sail around Africa discovered two groups of islands out in the Atlantic that they called the Azores, or Isles of Hawks, and the Canaries, or Isles of Dogs. When Columbus was in Portugal in 1470 he became acquainted with a young woman whose name was Philippa Perestrelo. In 1473 he married her.
Now Philippa's father, before his death, had been governor of Porto Santo, one of the Azores, and Columbus and his wife went off there to live. In the governor's house Columbus found a lot of charts and maps that told him about parts of the ocean that he had never before seen, and made him feel certain that he was right in saying that if he sailed away to the West he should find Cathay.
At that time there was an old man who lived in Florence, a city of Italy. His name was Toscanelli. He was a great scholar and studied the stars and made maps, and was a very wise man. Columbus knew what a wise old scholar Toscanelli was, for Florence is not very far from Genoa. So while he was living in the Azores he wrote to this old scholar asking him what he

thought about his idea that a man could sail around the world until he reached the land called the Indies and at last found Cathay.

Toscanelli wrote to Columbus saying that he believed his idea was the right one, and he said it would be a grand thing to do, if Columbus dared to try it. Perhaps, he said, you can find all those splendid things that I know are in Cathay—the great cities with marble bridges, the houses of marble covered with gold, the jewels and the spices and the precious stones, and all the other wonderful and magnificent things. I do not wonder you wish to try, he said, for if you find Cathay it will be a wonderful thing for you and for Portugal.

That settled it with Columbus. If this wise old scholar said he was right, he must be right. So he left his home in the Azores and went to Portugal. This was in 1475, and from that time on, for seventeen long years he was trying to get some king or prince to help him sail to the West to find Cathay.

But not one of the people who could have helped him, if they had really wished to, believed in Columbus. As I told you, they said that he was crazy. The king of Portugal, whose name was John, did a very unkind thing—I am sure you would call it a mean trick. Columbus had gone to him with his story and asked for ships and sailors. The king and his chief men refused to help him; but King John said to himself, perhaps there is something in this worth looking after and, if so, perhaps I can have my own people find Cathay and save the money that Columbus will want to keep for himself as his share of what he finds. So one day he copied off the sailing directions that Columbus had left with him, and gave them to one of his own captains without letting Columbus know anything about it, The Portuguese captain sailed away to the West in the direction Columbus had marked down, but a great storm came up and so frightened the sailors that they turned around in a hurry. Then they hunted up Columbus and began to abuse him for getting them into such a scrape. You might as well expect to find land in the sky, they said, as in those terrible waters.

And when, in this way, Columbus found out that King John had tried to use his ideas without letting him know anything about it, he was very angry. His wife had died in the midst of this mean trick of the Portuguese king, and so, taking with him his little five-year-old son, Diego, he left Portugal secretly and went over into Spain.

Near the little town of Palos, in western Spain, is a green hill looking out toward the Atlantic. Upon this hill stands an old building that, four hundred years ago, was used as a a convent or home for priests. It was called the Convent of Rabida, and the priest at the head of it was named the Friar Juan Perez. One autumn day, in the year 1484, Friar Juan Perez saw a dusty traveler with a little boy talking with the gate-keeper of the convent. The stranger was so tall and fine-looking, and seemed such an interesting man, that Friar Juan went out and began to talk with him. This man was Columbus.

As they talked, the priest grew more and more interested in what Columbus said. He invited him into the convent to stay for a few days, and he asked some other people—the doctor of Palos and some of the sea captains and sailors of the town—to come and talk with this stranger who had such a singular idea about sailing across the Atlantic.

It ended in Columbus's staying some months in Palos, waiting for a chance to go and see the king and queen. At last, in 1485, he set out for the Spanish court with a letter to a priest who was a friend of Friar Juan's, and who could help him to see the king and queen.

At that time the king and queen of Spain were fighting to drive out of Spain the people called the Moors. These people came from Africa, but they had lived in Spain for many years and had once been a very rich and powerful nation. They were not Spaniards; they were not Christians. So all

Spaniards and all Christians hated them and tried to drive them out of Europe.

The king and queen of Spain who were fighting the Moors were named Ferdinand and Isabella. They were pretty good people as kings and queens went in those days, but they did a great many very cruel and very mean things, just as the kings and queens of those days were apt to do. I am afraid we should not think they were very nice people nowadays. We certainly should not wish our American boys and girls to look up to them as good and true and noble.

When Columbus first came to them, they were with the army in the camp near the city of Cordova. The king and queen had no time to listen to what they thought were crazy plans, and poor Columbus could get no one to talk with him who could be of any help. So he was obliged to go back to drawing maps and selling books to make enough money to support himself and his little Diego.

But at last, through the friend of good Friar Juan Perez of Rabida, who was a priest at the court, and named Talavera, and to whom he had a letter of introduction, Columbus found a chance to talk over his plans with a number of priests and scholars in the city of Salamanca where there was a famous college and many learned men.

Columbus told his story. He said what he wished to do, and asked these learned men to say a good word for him to, Ferdinand and Isabella so that he could have the ships and sailors to sail to Cathay. But it was of no use.

What! sail away around the world? those wise men cried in horror. Why, you are crazy. The world is not round; it is flat. Your ships would tumble off the edge of the world and all the king's money and all the king's men would be lost. No, no; go away; you must not trouble the queen or even mention such a ridiculous thing again.

So the most of them said. But one or two thought it might be worth trying. Cathay was a very rich country, and if this foolish fellow were willing to run the risk and did succeed, it would be a good thing for Spain, as the king and queen would need a great deal of money after the war with the Moors was over. At any rate, it was a chance worth thinking about.

And so, although Columbus was dreadfully disappointed, he thought that if he had only a few friends at Court who were ready to say a good word for him he must not give up, but must try, try again. And so he staid in Spain.

CHAPTER III. HOW COLUMBUS GAINED A QUEEN FOR HIS FRIEND.

When you wish very much to do a certain thing it is dreadfully hard to be patient; it is harder still to have to wait. Columbus had to do both. The wars against the Moors were of much greater interest to the king and queen of Spain than was the finding of a new and very uncertain way to get to Cathay. If it had not been for the patience and what we call the persistence of Columbus, America would never have been discovered—at least not in his time.

He staid in Spain. He grew poorer and, poorer. He was almost friendless. It seemed as if his great enterprise must be given up. But he never lost hope. He never stopped trying. Even when he failed he kept on hoping and kept on trying. He felt certain that sometime he should succeed. As we have seen, he tried to interest the rulers of different countries, but with no success. He tried to get help from his old home-town of Genoa and failed; he tried Portugal and failed; he tried the Republic of Venice and failed; he tried the king and queen of Spain and failed; he tried some of the richest and most powerful of the nobles of Spain and failed; he tried the king of

England (whom he got his brother, Bartholomew Columbus, to go and see) and failed. There was still left the king of France. He would make one last attempt to win the king and queen of Spain to his side and if he failed with them he would try the last of the rulers of Western Europe, the king of France.

He followed the king and queen of Spain as they went from place to place fighting the Moors. He hoped that some day, when they wished to think of something besides fighting, they might think of him and the gold and jewels and spices of Cathay.

The days grew into months, the months to years, and still the war against the Moors kept on; and still Columbus waited for the chance that did not come. People grew to know him as "the crazy explorer" as they met him in the streets or on the church steps of Seville or Cordova, and even ragged little boys of the town, sharp-eyed and shrill-voiced as all such ragged little urchins are, would run after this big man with the streaming white hair and the tattered cloak, calling him names or tapping their brown little foreheads with their dirty fingers to show that even they knew that he was "as crazy as a loon."

At last he decided to make one more attempt before giving it up in Spain. His money was gone; his friends were few; but he remembered his acquaintances at Palos and so he journeyed back to see once more his good friend Friar Juan Perez at the Convent of Rabida on the hill that looked out upon the Atlantic he was so anxious to cross.

It was in the month of November, 1491, that he went back to the Convent of Rabida. If he could not get any encouragement there, he was determined to stay in Spain no longer but to go away and try the king of France.

Once more he talked over the finding of Cathay with the priests and the sailors of Palos. They saw how patient he was; how persistent he was; how he would never give up his ideas until he had tried them. They were moved by his determination. They began to believe in him more and more. They resolved to help him. One of the principal sea captains of Palos was named Martin Alonso Pinzon. He became so interested that he offered to lend Columbus money enough to make one last appeal to the king and queen of Spain, and if Columbus should succeed with them, this Captain Pinzon said that he would go into partnership with Columbus and help him out when it came to getting ready to sail to Cathay.

This was a move in the right direction. At once a messenger was sent to the splendid Spanish camp before the city of Granada, the last unconquered city of the Moors of Spain. The king and queen of Spain had been so long trying to capture Granada that this camp was really a city, with gates and walls and houses. It was called Santa Fe. Queen Isabella, who was in Santa Fe, after some delay, agreed to hear more about the crazy scheme of this persistent Genoese sailor, and the Friar Juan Perez was sent for. He talked so well in behalf of his friend Columbus that the queen became still more interested. She ordered Columbus to come and see her, and sent him sixty-five dollars to pay for a mule, a new suit of clothes and the journey to court.

About Christmas time, in the year 1491, Columbus, mounted upon his mule, rode into the Spanish camp before the city of Granada. But even now, when he had been told to come, he had to wait. Granada was almost captured; the Moors were almost conquered. At last the end came. On the second of January, 1492, the Moorish king gave up the keys of his beloved city, and the great Spanish banner was hoisted on the highest tower of the Alhambra—the handsomest building in Granada and one of the most beautiful in the world. The Moors were driven out of Spain and Columbus's chance had come.

So he appeared before Queen Isabella and her chief men and told them again of all his plans and desires. The queen and her advisers sat in a great room in that splendid Alhambra I have told you of. King Ferdinand was not there. He did not believe in Columbus and did not wish to let him have either money, ships or sailors to lose in such a foolish way. But as Columbus stood before her and talked so earnestly about how he expected to find the Indies and Cathay and what he hoped to bring away from there, Queen Isabella listened and thought the plan worth trying. Then a singular thing happened. You would think if you wished for something very much that you would give up a good deal for the sake of getting it. Columbus had worked and waited for seventeen years. He had never got what he wanted. He was always being disappointed. And yet, as he talked to the queen and told her what he wished to do, he said he must have so much as a reward for doing it that the queen and her chief men were simply amazed at his—well, what the boys to-day call "cheek"—that they would have nothing to do with him. This man really is crazy, they said. This poor Genoese sailor comes here without a thing except his very odd ideas, and almost "wants the earth" as a reward. This is not exactly what they said, but it is what they meant.

His few friends begged him to be more modest. Do not ask so much, they said, or you will get nothing. But Columbus was determined. I have worked and waited all these years, he replied. I know just what I can do and just how much I can do for the king and queen of Spain. They must pay me what I ask and promise what I say, or I will go somewhere else. Go, then! said the queen and her advisers. And Columbus turned his back on what seemed almost his last hope, mounted his mule and rode away.

Then something else happened. As Columbus rode off to find the French king, sick and tired of all his long and useless labor at the Spanish court, his few firm friends there saw that, unless they did something right away, all the glory and all the gain of this enterprise Columbus had taught them to believe in would be lost to Spain. So two of them, whose names were Santangel and Quintanilla, rushed into the queen's room and begged her, if she wished to become the greatest queen in Christendom, to call back this wandering sailor, agree to his terms and profit by his labors.

What if he does ask a great deal? they said. He has spent his life thinking his plan out; no wonder he feels that he ought to have a good share of what he finds. What he asks is really small compared with what Spain will gain. The war with the Moors has cost you ever so much; your money-chests are empty; Columbus will fill them up. The people of Cathay are heathen; Columbus will help you make them Christian men. The Indies and Cathay are full of gold and jewels; Columbus will bring you home shiploads of treasures. Spain has conquered the Moors; Columbus will help you conquer Cathay.

In fact, they talked to Queen Isabella so strongly and so earnestly, that she, too, became excited over this chance for glory and riches that she had almost lost, Quick! send for Columbus. Call him back! she said. I agree to his terms. If King Ferdinand cannot or will not take the risk, I, the queen, will do it all. Quick! do not let the man get into France. After him. Bring him back!

And without delay a royal messenger, mounted on a swift horse, was sent at full gallop to bring Columbus back.

All this time poor Columbus felt bad enough. Everything had gone wrong. Now he must go away into a new land and do it all over again. Kings and queens, he felt, were not to be depended upon, and he remembered a place in the Bible where it said: "Put not your trust in princes." Sad, solitary and heavy-hearted, he jogged slowly along toward the mountains, wondering what the king of France would say to him, and whether it was really worth trying.

Just as he was riding across the little bridge called the Bridge of Pinos, some six miles from Granada, he heard the quick hoof-beats of a horse behind him. It was a great spot for robbers, and Columbus felt of the little money he had in his traveling pouch, and wondered whether he must lose it all. The hoof-beats came nearer. Then a voice hailed him. Turn back, turn back! the messenger cried out. The queen bids you return to Granada. She grants you all you ask. Columbus hesitated. Ought he to trust this promise, he wondered. Put not your trust in princes, the verse in the Bible had said. If I go back I may only be put off and worried as I have been before. And yet, perhaps she means what she says. At any rate, I will go back and try once more. So, on the little Bridge of Pinos, he turned his mule around and rode back to Granada. And, sure enough, when he saw Queen Isabella she agreed to all that he asked. If he found Cathay, Columbus was to be made admiral for life of all the new seas and oceans into which he might sail; he was to be chief ruler of all the lands he might find; he was to keep one tenth part of all the gold and jewels and treasures he should bring away, and was to have his "say" in all questions about the new lands. For his part (and this was because of the offer of his friend at Palos, Captain Pinzon) he agreed to pay one eighth of all the expenses of this expedition and of all new enterprises, and was to have one eighth of all the profits from them.

So Columbus had his wish at last. The queen's men figured up how much money they could let him have; they called him "Don Christopher Columbus," "Your Excellency" and "Admiral," and at once he set about getting ready for his voyage.

CHAPTER IV. HOW THE ADMIRAL SAILED AWAY.

The agreement made between Columbus and the king and queen of Spain was signed on the seventeenth of April, 1492. But it was four months before he was quite ready to sail away.

He selected the town of Palos as the place to sail from, because there, as you know, Captain Pinzon lived; there, too, he had other acquaintances, so that he supposed it would be easy to get the sailors he needed for his ships. But in this he was greatly mistaken.

As soon as the papers had been signed that held the queen to her promise, Columbus set off for Palos. He stopped at the Convent of Rabida to tell the Friar Juan Perez how thankful he was to him for the help the good priest had given him, and how everything now looked promising and successful.

The town of Palos, as you can see from your map of Spain, is situated at the mouth of the river Tinto on a little bay in the southwestern part of Spain, not far from the borders of Portugal. To-day the sea has gone away from it so much that it is nearly high and dry; but four hundred years ago it was quite a seaport, when Spain did not have a great many sea towns on the Atlantic coast. At the time of Columbus's voyage the king and queen of Spain were angry with the port of Palos for something its people had done that was wrong—just what this was we do not know. But to punish the town, and because Columbus wished to sail from there, the king and queen ordered that Palos should pay them a fine for their wrong-doing. And this fine was to lend the king and queen of Spain, for one year, without pay, two sailing vessels of the kind called caravel's, armed and equipped "for the service of the crown"—that is, for the use of the king and queen of Spain, in the western voyage that Columbus was to make.

When Columbus called together the leading people of Palos to meet him in the church of St. George and hear the royal commands, they came; but at first they did not understand just what they must do. But when they knew that they must send two of their ships and some of their sailing men on this dreadful voyage far out upon the terrible Sea of Darkness, they were terribly distressed. Nobody was willing to go. They would obey the commands of the king and queen and furnish the two ships, but as for sailing off with this crazy sea captain—that they would not do. Then the king's officers went to work. They seized some sailors (impressed is the word for this), and made them go; they took some from the jails, and gave them their freedom as a reward for going; they begged and threatened and paid in advance, and still it was hard to get enough men for the two ships. Then Captain Pinzon, who had promised Columbus that he would join him, tried his hand. He added a third ship to the Admiral's "fleet." He made big promises to the sailors, and worked for weeks, until at last he was able to do what even the royal commands could not do, and a crew of ninety men was got together to man the three vessels. The names of these three vessels were the Capitana (changed before it sailed to the Santa Maria), the Pinta and the Nina or Baby. Captain de la Cosa commanded the Santa Maria, Captain Martin Alonso Pinzon the Pinta and his brother, Captain Vincent Pinzon, the Nina. The Santa Maria was the largest of the three vessels; it was therefore selected as the leader of the fleet—the flag-ship, as it is called—and upon it sailed the commander of the expedition, the Admiral Don Christopher Columbus.

When we think of a voyage across the Atlantic nowadays, we think of vessels as large as the big three-masted ships or the great ocean steamers—vessels over six hundred feet long and fifty feet wide. But these "ships" of Columbus were not really ships. They were hardly larger than the "fishing smacks" that sail up and down our coast to-day. Some of them were not so large. The Santa Maria was, as I have told you, the largest of the three, and she was only sixty-three feet long, twenty feet wide and ten and a half feet deep. Just measure this out on the ground and see how small, after all, the Admiral's "flag-ship" really was. The Pinta was even smaller than this, while the little Nina was hardly anything more than a good-sized sail boat. Do you wonder that the poor people of Palos and the towns round about were frightened when they thought of their fathers and brothers and sons putting out to sea, on the great ocean they had learned to dread so much, in such shaky little boats as these?

But finally the vessels were ready. The crews were selected. The time had come to go. Most of the sailors were Spanish men from the towns near to the sea, but somehow a few who were not Spaniards joined the crew.

One of the first men to land in America from one of the ships of Columbus was an Irishman named William, from the County Galway. And another was an Englishman named either Arthur Laws or Arthur Larkins. The Spanish names for both these men look very queer, and only a wise scholar who digs among names and words could have found out what they really were. But such a one did find it out, and it increases our interest in the discovery of America to know that some of our own northern blood—the Irishman and the Englishman—were in the crews of Columbus. The Admiral Columbus was so sure he was going to find a rich and civilized country, such as India and Cathay were said to be, that he took along on his ships the men he would need in such places as he expected to visit and among such splendid people as he was sure he should meet. He took along a lawyer to make out all the forms and proclamations and papers that would have to be sent by the Admiral to the kings and princes he expected to visit; he had a secretary and historian to write out the story of what he should find and what he should do. There was a learned Jew, named Louis, who could speak almost a dozen languages, and who could, of course, tell him what the people of Cathay and Cipango and the Indies were talking about. There was a jeweler and silversmith who knew all about the gold and silver and precious stones that Columbus was going to load the ships with; there was a doctor and a surgeon; there were cooks and pilots, and even a little fellow, who sailed in the Santa Maria as the Admiral's cabin boy, and whose name was Pedro de Acevedo.

Some scholars have said that it cost about two hundred and thirty thousand dollars to fit out this expedition. I do not think it cost nearly so much. We do know that Queen Isabella gave sixty-seven thousand dollars to help pay for it. Some people, however, reckoning the old Spanish money in a different way, say that what Queen Isabella gave toward the expedition was not over three or four thousand dollars of our money. Perhaps as much more was borrowed from King Ferdinand, although he was to have no share in the enterprise in which Queen Isabella and Columbus were partners.

It was just an hour before sunrise on Friday, the third of August, 1492, that the three little ships hoisted their anchors and sailed away from the port of Palos. I suppose it was a very sorry and a very exciting morning in Palos. The people probably crowded down on the docks, some of them sad and sorrowful, some of them restless and curious. Their fathers and brothers and sons and acquaintances were going—no one knew where, dragged off to sea by a crazy old Italian sailor who thought there was land to be found somewhere beyond the Jumping-off place. They all knew he was wrong. They were certain that nothing but dreadful goblins and horrible monsters lived off there to the West, just waiting to devour or destroy the poor sailors when these three little ships should tumble over the edge.

But how different Columbus must have felt as he stepped, into the rowboat that took him off to his "flag-ship," the Santa Maria. His dreams had come true. He had ships and sailors under his command, and was about to sail away to discover great and wonderful things. He who had been so poor that he could hardly buy his own dinner, was now called Don and Admiral. He had a queen for his friend and helper. He was given a power that only the richest and noblest could hope for. But more than all, he was to have the chance he had wished and worked for so long. He was to find the Indies; he was to see Cathay; he was to have his share in all the wealth he should discover and bring away. The son of the poor wool-weaver of Genoa was to be the friend of kings and princes; the cabin boy of a pirate was now Admiral of the Seas and Governor of the Colonies of Spain! Do you wonder that he felt proud?

So, as I have told you, just before sunrise on a Friday morning in August, he boarded the Santa Maria and gave orders to his captains "to get under way." The sailors with a "yo heave ho!" (or whatever the Spanish for that is) tugged at the anchors, the sails filled with the morning breeze, and while the people of Palos watched them from the shore, while the good friar, Juan Perez, raised his hands to Heaven calling down a blessing on the enterprise, while the children waved a last good-by from the water-stairs, the three vessels steered out from Palos Harbor, and before that day's sun had set, Columbus and his fleet were full fifty miles on their way across the Sea of Darkness. The westward voyage to those wonderful lands, the Indies and Cathay, had at last begun.

CHAPTER V. HOW THEY FARED ON THE SEA OF DARKNESS.

Did you ever set out, in the dark, to walk with your little brother or sister along a road you did not know much about or had never gone over before? It was not an easy thing to do, was it? And how did your little brother or sister feel when it was known that you were not just certain whether you were right or not? Do you remember what the Bible says about the blind leading the blind?

It was much the same with Columbus when he set out from Palos to sail over an unknown sea to find the uncertain land of Cathay. He had his own idea of the way there, but no one in all his company had ever sailed it, and he himself was not sure about it. He was very much in the dark. And the sailors in the three ships were worse than little children. They did not even have the confidence in their leader that your little brother or sister would probably have in you as you traveled that new road on a dark night. It was almost another case of the blind leading the blind, was it not?

Columbus first steered his ships to the south so as to reach the Canary Islands and commence his real westward voyage from there. The Canary Islands, as you will see by looking in your geography, are made up of seven islands and lie off the northern corner of Africa, some sixty miles or so west of Morocco. They were named Canaria by the Romans from the Latin canis, a dog, "because of the multitude of dogs of great size" that were found there. The canary birds that sing so sweetly in your home come from these islands. They had been known to the Spaniards and other European sailors of Columbus's day about a hundred years.

At the Canaries the troubles of Columbus commenced. And he did have a lot of trouble before his voyage was over. While near the island called the Grand Canary the rudder of the Pinta, in which Captain Alonso Pinzon sailed, somehow got loose, then broke and finally came off. It was said that two of the Pinta's crew, who were really the owners of the vessel, broke the rudder on purpose, because they had become frightened at the thoughts of the perilous voyage, and hoped by damaging their vessel to be left behind.

But Columbus had no thought of doing any such thing. He sailed to the island of Gomera, where he knew some people, and had the Pinta mended. And while lying here with his fleet the great mountain on the island of Teneriffe, twelve thousand feet high, suddenly began to spit out flame and smoke. It was, as of course you know, a volcano; but the poor frightened sailors did not know what set this mountain on fire, and they were scared almost out of their wits' and begged the Admiral to go back home. But Columbus would not. And as they sailed away from Gomera some sailors told them that the king of Portugal was angry with Columbus because he had got his ships from the king and queen of Spain, and that he had sent out some of his war-ships to worry or capture Columbus.

But these, too, Columbus escaped, although not before his crews had grown terribly nervous for fear of capture. At last they got away from the Canaries, and on Sunday, the ninth of September, 1492, with a fresh breeze filling their sails, the three caravels sailed away into the West. And as the shores of Ferro, the very last of the Canary Islands, faded out of sight, the sailors burst into sighs and murmurings and tears, saying that now indeed they were sailing off—off—off—upon the awful Sea of Darkness and would never see land any more.

When Columbus thought that he was sailing too slowly—he had now been away from Palos a month and was only about a hundred miles out at sea—and when he saw what babies his sailors were, he did something that was not just right (for it is never right to do anything that is not true) but which he felt he really must do. He made two records (or reckonings as they are called) of his sailing. One of these records was a true one; this he kept for himself. The other was a false one; this he kept to show his sailors. So while they thought they were sailing slowly and that the ocean was not so very wide, Columbus knew from his own true record that they were getting miles and miles away from home.

Soon another thing happened to worry the sailors. The pilots were steering by the compass. You know what that is—a sort of big magnet-needle perfectly balanced and pointing always to the north. At the time of Columbus the compass was a new thing and was only understood by a few. On the thirteenth of September they had really got into the middle of the ocean, and the line of the north changed. Of course this made the needle in the compass change its position also. Now the sailors had been taught to believe so fully in the compass that they thought it could never change its position. And here it was playing a cruel trick upon them. We are trapped! they cried. The goblins in this dreadful sea are making our compass point wrong so as to drag us to destruction. Go back; take us back! they demanded.

But Columbus, though he knew that his explanation was wrong, said the compass was all right. The North Star, toward which the needle always pointed, had, so he said, changed its position. This quieted the sailors for a while.

When they had been about forty days out from Palos, the ship ran into what is marked upon your maps as the Sargasso Sea. This is a vast meadow of floating seaweed and seagrass in the middle of the Atlantic; it is kept drifting about in the same place by the two great sea currents that flow past it but not through it.

The sailors did not know this, of course, and when the ships began to sail slower and slower because the seaweed was so thick and heavy and because there was no current to carry them along, they were sure that they were somewhere near to the jumping-off place, and that the horrible monsters they had heard of were making ready to stop their ships, and when they had got them all snarled up in this weed to drag them all down to the bottom of the sea.

For nearly a week the ships sailed over these vast sea-meadows, and when they were out of them they struck what we call the trade-winds—a never-failing breeze that blew them ever westward. Then the sailors cried out that they were in an enchanted land where there was but one wind and never a breeze to blow the poor sailors home again. Were they not fearfully "scarey?" But no doubt we should have been so, too, if we had been with them and knew no more than they did.

And when they had been over fifty days from home on the twenty-fifth of September, some one suddenly cried Land! Land! And all hands crowded to the side. Sure enough, they all saw it, straight ahead of them—fair green islands and lofty hills and a city with castles and temples and palaces that glittered beautifully in the sun.

Then they all cried for joy and sang hymns of praise and shouted to each other that their troubles were over. Cathay, it is Cathay! they cried; and they steered straight for the shining city. But, worst of all their troubles, even as they sailed toward the land they thought to be Cathay, behold! it all disappeared—island and castle and palace and temple and city, and nothing but the tossing sea lay all about them.

For this that they had seen was what is called a mirage—a trick of the clouds and the sun and the sea that makes people imagine they see what they would like to, but really do not. But after this Columbus had a harder time than ever with his men, for they were sure he was leading them all astray.

And so with frights and imaginings and mysteries like these, with strange birds flying about the ships and floating things in the water that told of land somewhere about them, with hopes again and again disappointed, and with the sailors growing more and more restless and discontented, and muttering threats against this Italian adventurer who, was leading the ships and sailors of the Spanish king to sure destruction, Columbus still sailed on, as full of patience and of faith, as certain of success as he had ever been.

On the seventh of October, 1492, the true record that Columbus was keeping showed that he had sailed twenty-seven hundred miles from the Canaries; the false record that the sailors saw said they had sailed twenty-two hundred miles. Had Columbus kept straight on, he would have landed very soon upon the coast of Florida or South Carolina, and would really have discovered the mainland of America. But Captain Alonso Pinzon saw what looked like a flock of parrots flying south. This made him think the land lay that way; so he begged the Admiral to change his course to the southward as he was sure there was no land to the west. Against his will, Columbus at last consented, and turning to the southwest headed for Cuba.

But he thought he was steering for Cathay. The islands of Japan, were, he thought, only a few leagues away to the west. They were really, as you know, away across the United States and then across the Pacific Ocean, thousands of miles farther west than Columbus could sail. But according to his reckoning he hoped within a day or two to see the cities and palaces of this wonderful land.

When they sailed from the Canaries a reward had been offered to whomsoever should first see land. This reward was to be a silken jacket and nearly five hundred dollars in money; so all the sailors were on the watch.

At about ten o'clock on the evening of the eleventh of October, Columbus, standing on the high raised stern of the Santa Maria, saw a moving light, as if some one on the shore were running with a flaming torch. At two o'clock the next morning—Friday, the twelfth of October, 1492 the sharp eyes of a watchful sailor on the Pinta (his name was Rodrigo de Triana) caught sight of a long low coastline not far away. He raised the joyful shout Land, ho! The ships ran in as near to the shore as they dared, and just ten weeks after the anchors had been hauled up in Palos Harbor they were dropped overboard, and the hips of Columbus were anchored in the waters of a new world.

Where was it? What was it? Was it Cathay? Columbus was sure that it was. He was certain that the morning sun would shine for him upon the marble towers and golden roofs of the wonderful city of the kings of Cathay.

CHAPTER VI. WHAT COLUMBUS DISCOVERED.

A little over three hundred years ago there was a Pope of Rome whose name was Gregory XIII. He was greatly interested in learning and science, and when the scholars and wise men of his day showed him that a mistake in reckoning time had long before been made he set about to make it right. At that time the Pope of Rome had great influence with the kings and queens of Europe, and whatever he wished them to do they generally did.

So they all agreed to his plan of renumbering the days of the year, and a new reckoning of time was made upon the rule that most of you know by heart in the old rhyme:

Thirty days hath September, April, June and November; All the rest have thirty-one, Excepting February which alone Hath twenty-eight—and this, in fine, One year in four hath twenty-nine. And the order of the days of the months and the year is what is called, after Pope Gregory, the Gregorian Calendar.

This change in reckoning time made, of course, all past dates wrong. The old dates, which were called Old Style, had to be made to correspond with the new dates which were called New Style. Now, according to the Old Style, Columbus discovered the islands he thought to be the Indies (and which have ever since been called the West Indies) on the twelfth of October, 1492. But, according to the New Style, adopted nearly one hundred years after his discovery, the right date would be the twenty-first of October. And this is why, in the Columbian memorial year of 1892, the world celebrated the four hundredth anniversary of the discovery of America on the twenty-first of October; which, as you see, is the same as the twelfth under the Old Style of reckoning time.

But did Columbus discover America? What was this land that greeted his eyes as the daylight came on that Friday morning, and he saw the low green shores that lay ahead of his caravels. As far as Columbus was concerned he was sure that he had found some one of the outermost islands of Cipango or Japan. So he dropped his anchors, ordered out his rowboat, and prepared to take possession of the land in the name of the queen of Spain, who had helped him in his enterprise.

Just why or by what right a man from one country could sail up to the land belonging to another country and, planting in the ground the flag of his king, could say, "This land belongs to my king!" is a hard question to answer. But there is an old saying that tells us, Might makes right; and the servants of the kings and queens—the adventurers and explorers of old—used to go sailing about the world with this idea in their heads, and as soon as they came to a land they, had never seen before, up would go their flag, and they would say, This land is mine and my king's! They would not of course do this in any of the well-known or "Christian lands" of Europe; but they believed that all "pagan lands" belonged by right to the first European king whose sailors should discover and claim them.

So Columbus lowered a boat from the Santa Maria, and with two of his chief men and some sailors for rowers he pulled off toward the island.

But before he did so, he had to listen to the cheers and congratulations of the very sailors who, only a few days before, were ready to kill him. But, you see, this man whom they thought crazy had really brought them to the beautiful land, just as he had promised. It does make such a difference, you know, in what people say whether a thing turns out right or not.

Columbus, as I say, got into his rowboat with his chief inspector and his lawyer. He wore a crimson cloak over his armor, and in his hand he held the royal banner of Spain. Following him came Captain Alonso Pinzon in a rowboat from the Pinta, and in a rowboat from the Nina Captain Vincent Pinzon. Each of these captains carried the "banner of the green cross" on which were to be seen the initials of the king and queen of Spain.

As they rowed toward the land they saw some people on the shore. They were not dressed in the splendid clothes the Spaniards expected to find the people of Cathay wearing. In fact, they did not have on much of anything but grease and paint. And the land showed no signs of the marble temples and gold-roofed palaces the sailors expected to find. It was a little, low, flat green island, partly covered with trees and with what looked like a lake in the center.

This land was, in fact, one of the three thousand keys or coral islands that stretch from the capes of Florida to the island of Hayti, and are known as the Bahama Islands. The one upon which Columbus landed was called by the natives Guanahani, and was either the little island now marked on the map as Cat Island or else the one called Watling's Island. Just which of these it was has been discussed over and over again, but careful scholars have now but little doubt that it was the one known to-day as Watling's Island. To see no sign of glittering palaces and gayly dressed people was quite a disappointment to Columbus. But then, he said, this, is probably the island farthest out to sea, and the people who live here are not the real Cathay folks. We shall see them very soon.

So with the royal banner and the green-cross standards floating above him, with his captains and chief officers and some of the sailors gathered about him, while all the others watched him from the decks of his fleet, Columbus stepped upon the shore. Then he took off his hat, and holding the royal banner in one hand and his sword in the other he said aloud: I take possession of this island, which I name San Salvador,(*) and of all the islands and lands about it in the name of my patron and sovereign lady, Isabella, and her kingdom of Castile. This, or something like it, he said, for the exact words are not known to us.

(*) The island of San Salvador means the island of the Holy Saviour. Columbus and the Spanish explorers who followed him gave Bible or religious names to very much of the land they discovered.

And when he had done this the captains and sailors fell at his feet in wonder and admiration, begging him to forgive them for all the hard things they had said about him. For you have found Cathay, they cried. You are our leader. You will make us rich and powerful. Hurrah for the great Admiral!

And when the naked and astonished people of the island saw all this—the canoes with wings, as they called the ships, the richly-dressed men with white and bearded faces, the flags and swords, and the people kneeling about this grand-looking old man in the crimson cloak—they said to one another: These men are gods; they have come from Heaven to see us. And then, they, too, fell on the ground and worshiped these men from Heaven, as they supposed Columbus and his sailors to be.

And when they found that the men from Heaven did not offer to hurt them, they came nearer; and the man in the crimson cloak gave them beads and pieces of bright cloth and other beautiful things they had never seen before. And this made them feel all the more certain that these men who had come to see them in the canoes with wings must really be from Heaven. So they brought them fruits and flowers and feathers and birds as presents; and both parties, the men with clothes and the men without clothes, got on very well together.

But Columbus, as we know, had come across the water for one especial reason. He was to find Cathay, and he was to find it so that he could carry back to Spain the gold and jewels and spices of Cathay. The first thing, therefore, that he tried to find out from the people of the island—whom he called "Indians," because he thought he had come to a part of the coast of India was where Cathay might be.

Of course they did not understand him. Even Louis, the interpreter, who knew a dozen languages and who tried them all, could not make out what these "Indians" said. But from their signs and actions and from the sound of the words they spoke, Columbus understood that Cathay was off somewhere to the southwest, and that the gold he was bound to find came from there. The "Indians" had little bits of gold hanging in their ears and noses. So Columbus supposed that among the finer people he hoped soon to meet in the southwest, he should find great quantities of the yellow metal. He was delighted. Success, he felt, was not far off. Japan was near, China was near, India was near. Of this he was certain; and even until he died Columbus did not have any idea that he had found a new world—such as America really was. He was sure that he had simply landed upon the eastern coasts of Asia and that he had found what he set out to discover—the nearest route to the Indies.

The next day Columbus pulled up his anchors, and having seized and carried off to his ships some of the poor natives who had welcomed him so gladly, he commenced a cruise among the islands of the group he had discovered.

Day after day he sailed among these beautiful tropic islands, and of them and of the people who lived upon them he wrote to the king and queen of Spain: "This country excels all others as far as the day surpasses the night in splendor. The natives love their neighbors as themselves; their conversation is the sweetest imaginable; their faces smiling; and so gentle and so affectionate are they, that I swear to Your Highness there is not a better people in the world."

Does it not seem a pity that so great a man should have acted so meanly toward these innocent people who loved and trusted him so? For it was Columbus who first stole them away from their island homes and who first thought of making them slaves to the white men.

CHAPTER VII. HOW A BOY BROUGHT THE ADMIRAL TO GRIEF.

Columbus kept sailing on from one island to another. Each new island he found would, he hoped, bring him nearer to Cathay and to the marble temples and golden palaces and splendid cities he was looking for. But the temples and palaces and cities did not appear. When the Admiral came to the coast of Cuba he said: This, I know, is the mainland of Asia. So he sent off Louis, the interpreter, with a letter to the "great Emperor of Cathay." Louis was gone several days; but he found no emperor, no palace, no city, no gold, no jewels, no spices, no Cathay— only frail houses of bark and reeds, fields of corn and grain, with simple people who could tell him nothing about Cathay or Cipango or the Indies.

So day after day Columbus kept on his search, sailing from island to island, getting a little gold here and there, or some pearls and silver and a lot of beautiful bird skins, feathers and trinkets. Then Captain Alonso Pinzon, who was sailing in the Pinta, believed he could do better than follow the Admiral's lead. I know, he said, if I could go off on my own hook I could find plenty of gold and pearls, and perhaps I could find Cathay. So one day he sailed away and Columbus did not know what had become of him.

At last Columbus, sailing on and troubled at the way Captain Alonso Pinzon had acted, came one day to the island of Hayti. If Cuba was Cathay (or China), Hayti, he felt sure, must be Cipango (or Japan). So he decided to sail into one of its harbors to spend Christmas Day. But just before Christmas morning dawned, the helmsman of the Santa Maria, thinking that everything was safe, gave the tiller into the hands of a boy—perhaps it was little Pedro the cabin boy—and went to sleep. The rest of the crew also were asleep. And the boy who, I suppose, felt quite big to think that he was really steering the Admiral's flagship, was a little too smart; for, before he knew it, he had driven the Santa Maria plump upon a hidden reef. And there she was wrecked. They worked hard to get her off but it was no use. She keeled over on her side, her seams opened, the water leaked in, the waves broke over her, the masts fell out and the Santa Maria had made her last voyage.

Then Columbus was in distress. The Pinta had deserted him, the Santa Maria was a wreck, the Nina was not nearly large enough to carry all his men back to Spain. And to Spain he must return at once. What should he do?

Columbus was quick at getting out of a fix. So in this case he speedily decided what to do. He set his men at work tearing the wreck of the Santa Maria to pieces. Out of her timbers and woodwork, helped out with trees from the woods and a few stones from the shore, he made quite a fort. It had a ditch and a watch-tower and a drawbridge. It proudly floated the flag of Spain. It was the first European fort in the new world. On its ramparts Columbus mounted the cannons he had saved from the wreck and named the fort La Navidad—that is, Fort Nativity, because it was made out of the ship that was wrecked on Christmas Day-the day of Christ's nativity, his birthday.

He selected forty of his men to stay in the fort until he should return from Spain. The most of them were quite willing to do this as they thought the place was a beautiful one and they would be kept very busy filling the fort with gold. Columbus told them they must have at least a ton of gold before he came back. He left them provisions and powder for a year, he told them to be careful and watchful, to be kind to the Indians and to make the year such a good one that the king and queen of Spain would be glad to reward them. And then he said good-by and sailed away for Spain.

It was on the fourth of January, 1493, that Columbus turned the little Nina homeward. He had not sailed very far when what should he come across but the lost Pinta. Captain Alonso Pinzon seemed very much ashamed when he saw the Admiral, and tried to explain his absence. Columbus knew well enough that Captain Pinzon had gone off gold hunting and had not found any gold. But he did not scold him, and both the vessels sailed toward Spain.

The homeward voyage was a stormy and seasick one. Once it was so rough that Columbus thought surely the Nina would be wrecked. So he copied off the story of what he had seen and done, addressed it to the king and queen of Spain, put it into a barrel and threw the barrel overboard.

But the Nina was not shipwrecked, and on the eighteenth of February Columbus reached the Azores. The Portuguese governor was so surprised when he heard this crazy Italian really had returned, and was so angry to think it was Spain and not Portugal that was to profit by his voyage that he tried to make Columbus a prisoner. But the Admiral gave this inhospitable welcomer the slip and was soon off the coast of Portugal.

Here he was obliged to land and meet the king of Portugal—that same King John who had once acted so meanly toward him. King John would have done so again had he dared. But things were quite different now. Columbus was a great man. He had made a successful voyage, and the king and queen of Spain would have made it go hard with the king of Portugal if he dared trouble their admiral. So King John had to give a royal reception to Columbus, and permit him to send a messenger to the king and queen of Spain with the news of his return from Cathay.

Then Columbus went on board the Nina again and sailed for Palos. But his old friend Captain Alonso Pinzon had again acted badly. For he had left the Admiral in one of the storms at sea and had hurried homeward. Then he sailed into one of the northern ports of Spain, and hoping to get all the credit for his voyage, sent a messenger post-haste to the king and queen with the word that he had returned from Cathay and had much to tell them. And then he, too, sailed for Palos.

On the fifteenth of March, 1493, just seven months after he had sailed away to the West, Columbus in the Nina sailed into Palos Harbor. The people knew the little vessel at once. And then what a time they made! Columbus has come back, they cried. He has found Cathay. Hurrah! hurrah! And the bells rang and the cannons boomed and the streets were full of people. The sailors were welcomed with shouts of joy, and the big stories they told were listened to with open mouths and many exclamations of surprise. So Columbus came back to Palos. And everybody pointed him out and cheered him and he was no longer spoken of as "that crazy Italian who dragged away the men of Palos to the Jumping-off place."

And in the midst of all this rejoicing what should sail into the harbor of Palos but the Pinta, just a few hours late! And when Captain Alonso Pinzon heard the sounds of rejoicing, and knew that his plans to take away from Columbus all the glory of what had been done had all gone wrong, he did not even go to see his old friend and ask his pardon. He went away to his own house without seeing any one. And there he found a stern letter from the king and queen of Spain scolding him for trying to get the best of Columbus, and refusing to hear or see him. The way things had turned out made Captain Alonso Pinzon feel so badly that he fell sick; and in a few days he died.

But Columbus, after he had seen his good friend Juan Perez, the friar at Rabida, and told him all his adventures, went on to Barcelona where King Ferdinand and Queen Isabella were waiting for him. They had already sent him letters telling him how pleased they were that he had found

Cathay, and ordering him to get ready for a second expedition at once. Columbus gave his directions for this, and then, in a grand procession that called everybody to the street or window or housetop, he set off for Barcelona. He reached the court on a fine April day and was at once received with much pleasure by the king and queen of Spain.

Columbus told them where he had been and what he had seen; he showed them the gold and the pearls and the birds and curiosities he had brought to Spain as specimens, of what was to be found in Cathay; he showed them the ten painted and "fixed-up" Indians he had stolen and brought back with him.

And the king and queen of Spain said he had done well. They had him sit beside them while he told his story, and treated this poor Italian wool-weaver as they would one of their great princes or mighty lords. They told him he could put the royal arms alongside his own on his shield or crest, and they bade him get together at once ships and sailors for a second expedition to Cathay—ships and sailors enough, they said, to get away up to the great cities of Cathay, where the marble temples and the golden palaces must be. It was their wish, they said, to gain the friendship of the great Emperor of Cathay, to trade with him and get a good share of his gold and jewels and spices. For, you see, no one as yet imagined that Columbus had discovered America. They did not even know that there was such a continent. They thought he had sailed to Asia and found the rich countries that Marco Polo had told such big stories about.

Columbus, you may be sure, was "all the rage" now. Wherever he went the people followed him, cheering and shouting, and begging him to take them with him on his next voyage to Cathay. He was as anxious as any one to get back to those beautiful islands and hunt for gold and jewels. He set to work at once, and on the twenty-fifth of September, 1493, with a fleet of seventeen ships and a company of fifteen hundred men, Columbus the Admiral set sail from Cadiz on his second voyage to Cathay and Cipango and the Indies. And this time he was certain he should find all these wonderful places, and bring back from the splendid cities unbounded wealth for the king and queen of Spain.

CHAPTER VIII. TRYING IT AGAIN.

Do you not think Columbus must have felt very fine as he sailed out of Cadiz Harbor on his second voyage to the West? It was just about a year before, you know, that his feeble fleet of three little ships sailed from Palos port. His hundred sailors hated to go; his friends were few; everybody else said he was crazy; his success was very doubtful. Now, as he stood on the high quarter-deck of his big flag-ship, the Maria Galante, he was a great man. By appointment of his king and queen he was "Admiral of the Ocean Seas" and "Viceroy of the Indies." He had servants, to do as he directed; he had supreme command over the seventeen ships of his fleet, large and small; fifteen hundred men joyfully crowded his decks, while thousands left at home wished that they might go with him, too. He had soldiers and sailors, horsemen and footmen; his ships were filled with all the things necessary for trading with the Indians and the great merchants of Cathay, and for building the homes of those who wished to live in the lands beyond the sea.

Everything looked so well and everybody was so full of hope and expectation that the Admiral felt that now his fondest dreams were coming to pass and that he was a great man indeed.

This was to be a hunt for gold. And so sure of success was Columbus that he promised the king and queen of Spain, out of the money he should make on this voyage, to, himself pay for the fitting out of a great army of fifty thousand foot soldiers and four thousand horsemen to drive away the pagan Turks who had captured and held possession of the city of Jerusalem and the sepulcher of Christ. For this had been the chief desire, for years and years, of the Christian people of Europe. To accomplish it many brave knights and warriors had fought and failed. But now Columbus was certain he could do it.

So, out into the western ocean sailed the great expedition of the Admiral. He sailed first to the Canary Isles, where he took aboard wood and water and many cattle, sheep and swine. Then, on the seventeenth of October, he steered straight out into the broad Atlantic, and on Sunday, the third of November, he saw the hill-tops of one of the West India Islands that he named Dominica. You can find it on your map of the West Indies.

For days he sailed on, passing island after island, landing on some and giving them names. Some of them were inhabited, some of them were not; some were very large, some were very small. But none of them helped him in any way to find Cathay, so at last he steered toward Hayti (or Hispaniola, as he called it) and the little ship-built fortress of La Navidad, where his forty comrades had been left.

On the twenty-seventh of November, the fleet of the Admiral cast anchor off the solitary fort. It was night. No light was to be seen on the shore; through the darkness nothing could be made out that looked like the walls of the fort. Columbus fired a cannon; then he fired another. The echoes were the only answer. They must be sound sleepers in our fortress there, said the Admiral. At last, over the water he heard the sound of oars—or was it the dip of a paddle? A voice called for the Admiral; but it was not a Spanish voice. The interpreter—who was the only one left of those ten stolen Indians carried by Columbus to Spain—came to the Admiral's side; by the light of the ship's lantern they could make out the figure of an Indian in his canoe. He brought presents from his chief. But where are my men at the fort? asked the Admiral. And then the whole sad story was told.

The fort of La Navidad was destroyed; the Spaniards were all dead; the first attempt of Spain to start a colony in the new world was a terrible failure. And for it the Spaniards themselves were to blame.

After Columbus had left them, the forty men in the fort did not do as he told them or as they had solemnly promised. They were lazy; they were rough; they treated the Indians badly; they quarreled among themselves; some of them ran off to live in the woods. Then sickness came; there were two "sides," each one jealous of the other; the Indians became enemies. A fiery war-chief from the hills, whose name was Caonabo, led the Indians against the white men. The fort and village were surprised, surrounded and destroyed. And the little band of "conquerors"—as the Spaniards loved to call themselves—was itself conquered and killed.

It was a terrible disappointment to Columbus. The men in whom he had trusted had proved false. The gold he had told them to get together they had not even found. His plans had all gone wrong. But Columbus was not the man to stay defeated. His fort was destroyed, his men were killed, his settlement was a failure. It can't be helped now, he said. I will try again.

This time he would not only build a fort, he would build a city. He had men and material enough to do this and to do it well. So he set to work.

But the place where he had built from the wreck of the unlucky Santa Maria his unlucky fort of La Navidad did not suit him. It was low, damp and unhealthy. He must find a better place. After looking about for some time he finally selected a place on the northern side of the island. You can find it if you look at the map of Hayti in the West Indies; it is near to Cape Isabella.

He found here a good harbor for ships, a good place on the rocks for a fort, and good land for gardens. Here Columbus laid out his new town, and called it after his friend the queen of Spain, the city of Isabella.

He marked out a central spot for his park or square; around this ran a street, and along this street he built large stone buildings for a storehouse, a church and a house for himself, as governor of the colony. On the side streets were built the houses for the people who were to live in the new town, while on a rocky point with its queer little round tower looking out to sea stood the stone fort to protect the little city. It was the first settlement made by white men in all the great new world of America.

You must know that there are some very wise and very bright people who do not agree to this. They say that nearly five hundred years before Columbus landed, a Norwegian prince or viking, whose name was Leif Ericsson, had built on the banks of the beautiful Charles River, some twelve miles from Boston, a city which he called Norumbega.

But this has not really been proved. It is almost all the fancy of a wise man who has studied it out for himself, and says he believes there was such a city. But he does not really know it as we know of the city of Isabella, and so we must still say that Christopher Columbus really discovered America and built the first fort and the first city on its shores—although he thought he was doing all this in Asia, on the shores of China or Japan.

When Columbus had his people nearly settled in their new city of Isabella, he remembered that the main thing he was sent to do was to get together as much gold as possible. His men were already grumbling. They had come over the sea, they said, not to dig cellars and build huts, but to find gold—gold that should make them rich and great and happy.

So Columbus set to work gold-hunting. At first things seemed to promise success. The Indians told big stories of gold to be found in the mountains of Hayti; the men sent to the mountains discovered signs of gold, and at once Columbus sent home joyful tidings to the king and queen of Spain.

Then he and his men hunted everywhere for the glittering yellow metal. They fished for it in the streams; they dug for it in the earth; they drove the Indians to hunt for it also until the poor redmen learned to hate the very sound of the word gold, and believed that this was all the white men lived for, cared for or worked for; holding up a piece of this hated gold the Indians would say, one to another: "Behold the Christian's god!" And so it came about that the poor worried natives, who were not used to such hard work, took the easiest way out of it all, and told the Spaniards the biggest kind of lies as to where gold might be found—always away off somewhere else—if only the white men would go there to look for it.

On the thirteenth of January, 1494, Columbus sent back to Spain twelve of his seventeen ships. He did not send back in them to the king, and queen, the gold he had promised. He sent back the letters that promised gold; he sent back as prisoners for punishment some of the most discontented and quarrelsome of his colonists; and, worst of all, he sent to the king and queen a note asking, them to permit him to send to Spain all the Indians he could catch, to be sold as slaves. He said that by doing this they could make "good Christians" of the Indians, while the money that came from selling the natives would buy cattle for the colony and leave some money for the royal money-chests.

It is not pleasant to think this of so great a man as Columbus. But it is true, and he is really the man who, started the slave-trade in America. Of course things were very different in his time from what they are to-day, and people did not think so badly of this horrible business. But some good men did, and spoke out boldly against it. What they said was not of much use, however, and slavery was started in the new world. And from that act of Columbus came much sorrow and trouble for the land he found. Even the great war between the northern and southern sections of our own United States, upon one side or the other of which your fathers, or your grandfathers perhaps, fought with gun and sword, was brought about by this act of the great Admiral Columbus hundreds of years before.

So the twelve ships sailed back to Spain, and Columbus, with his five remaining ships, his soldiers and his colonists, remained in the new city of Isabella to keep up the hunt for gold or to become farmers in the new world.

CHAPTER IX. HOW THE TROUBLES OF THE ADMIRAL BEGAN.

Both the farmers and the gold hunters had a hard time of it in the land they had come to so hopefully. The farmers did not like to farm when they thought they could do so much better at gold hunting; the gold hunters found that it was the hardest kind of work to get from the water or pick from the rocks the yellow metal they were so anxious to obtain.

Columbus himself was not satisfied with the small amount of gold he got from the streams and mines of Hayti; he was tired of the wrangling and grumbling of his men. So, one day, he hoisted sail on his five ships and started away on a hunt for richer gold mines, or, perhaps, for those wonderful cities of Cathay he was still determined to find.

He sailed to the south and discovered the island of Jamaica. Then he coasted along the shores of Cuba. The great island stretched away so many miles that Columbus was certain it was the mainland of Asia. There was some excuse for this mistake. The great number of small islands he had sailed by all seemed to lie just as the books about Cathay that he had read said they did; the trees and fruits that he found in these islands seemed to be just the same that travelers said grew in Cathay.

To be sure the marble temples, the golden-roofed palaces, the gorgeous cities had not yet appeared; but Columbus was so certain that he had found Asia that he made all his men sign a paper in which they declared that the land they had found (which was, as you know, the island of Cuba) was really and truly the coast of Asia.

This did not make it so, of course; but it made the people of Spain, and the king and queen, think it was so. And this was most important. So, to keep the sailors from going back on their word and the statement they had signed, Columbus ordered that if any officer should afterward say he had been mistaken, he should be fined one hundred dollars; and if any sailor should say so, he should receive one hundred lashes with a whip and have his tongue pulled out. That was a curious way to discover Cathay, was it not?

Then Columbus, fearing another shipwreck or another mutiny, sailed back again to the city of Isabella. His men were discontented, his ships were battered and leaky, his hunt for gold and palaces had again proved a failure. He sailed around Jamaica; he got as far as the eastern end of Hayti, and then, just as he was about to run into the harbor of Isabella, all his strength gave out. The strain and the disappointment were too much for him; he fell very, very sick, and on the twenty-ninth of September, 1494, after just about five months of sailing and wandering and hunting, the Nina ran into Isabella Harbor with Columbus so sick from fever that he could not raise his hand or his head to give an order to his men.

For five long months Columbus lay in his stone house on the plaza or square of Isabella a very sick man. His brother Bartholomew had come across from Spain with three supply ships,

bringing provisions for the colony. So Bartholomew took charge of affairs for a while.
And while Columbus lay so sick, some of the leading men in the colony seized the ships in which Bartholomew Columbus had come to his brother's aid, and sailing back to Spain they told the king and queen all sorts of bad stories about Columbus. They were Spaniards. Columbus was an Italian. They were jealous of him because he was higher placed and had more to say than they had. They were angry to think that when he had promised to bring them to the gorgeous cities and the glittering gold mines of Cathay he had only landed them on islands which were the homes of naked savages, and made them work dreadfully hard for what little gold they could find. He had promised them power; they went home poorer than when they came away. So they were "mad" at Columbus—just as boys and girls are sometimes "mad" at one another; and they told the worst stories they could think of about him, and called him all sorts of hard names, and said the king and queen of Spain ought to look out for "their great Admiral," or he would get the best of them and keep for himself the most of whatever he could find in the new lands.
At last Columbus began to grow better. And when he knew what his enemies had done he was very much troubled for fear they should get the king and queen to refuse him any further aid. So, just as soon as he was able, on the tenth of March, 1496, he sailed home to Spain.
How different was this from his splendid setting out from Cadiz two years before. Then everything looked bright and promising; now everything seemed dark and disappointing. The second voyage to the Indies had been a failure.
So, tired of his hard work in trying to keep his dissatisfied men in order, in trying to check the Indians who were no longer his friends, in trying to find the gold and pearls that were to be got at only by hard work, in trying to make out just where he was and just where Cathay might be, Columbus started for home. Sick, troubled, disappointed, threatened by enemies in the Indies and by more bitter enemies at home, sad, sorry and full of fear, but yet as determined and as brave as ever, on the tenth of March, 1496, he went on board his caravels with two hundred and fifty homesick and feversick men, and on the eleventh of June his two vessels sailed into the harbor of Cadiz.
The voyage had been a tedious one. Short of food, storm-tossed and full of aches and pains the starving company "crawled ashore," glad to be in their home land once more, and most of them full of complaints and grumblings at their commander, the Admiral.
And Columbus felt as downcast as any. He came ashore dressed, not in the gleaming armor and crimson robes of a conqueror, as on his first return, but in the garb of what was known as a penitent—the long, coarse gown, the knotted girdle and peaked hood of a priest. For, you see, he did not know just what terrible stories had been told by his enemies; he did not know how the king and queen would receive him. He had promised them so much; he had brought them so little. He had sailed away so hopefully; he had come back humbled and hated. The greatest man in the world, he had been in 1492; and in 1496 he was unsuccessful, almost friendless and very unpopular. So you see, boys and girls, that success is a most uncertain thing, and the man who is a hero to-day may be a beggar to-morrow.
But, as is often the case, Columbus was too full of fear. He was not really in such disgrace as he thought he was. Though his enemies had said all sorts of hard things against him, the king—and especially the queen—could not forget that he was, after all, the man who, had found the new land for Spain; they knew that even though he had not brought home the great riches that were to have been gathered in the Indies, he had still found for Spain a land that would surely, in time, give to it riches, possessions and power.
So they sent knightly messengers to Columbus telling him to come and see them at once, and

greeting him with many pleasant and friendly words. Columbus was, as you must have seen, quick to feel glad again the moment things seemed to turn in his favor; so he laid aside his penitent's gown, and hurried off to court. And almost the first thing he did was to ask the king and queen to fit out another fleet for him. Six ships, he said he should want this time; and with these he was certain he could sail into the yet undiscovered waters that lay beyond Hayti and upon which he knew he should find Cathay.

I am afraid the king and queen of Spain were beginning to feel a little doubtful as to this still undiscovered Cathay. At any rate, they had other matters to think of and they did not seem so very anxious to spend more money on ships and sailors. But they talked very nicely to Columbus; they gave him a new title (this time it was duke or marquis); they made him a present of a great tract of land in Hayti, but it was months and months before they would help him with the ships and money he kept asking for.

At last, however, the queen, Isabella, who had always had more interest in Columbus and his plans than had the king, her husband, said a good word for him. The six ships were given him, men and supplies were put on board and on the twentieth of May, 1498, the Admiral set out on his third voyage to what every one now called the Indies.

There was not nearly so much excitement among the people about this voyage. Cathay and its riches had almost become an old story; at any rate it was a story that was not altogether believed in. Great crowds did not now follow the Admiral from place to place begging him to take them with him to the Indies. The hundreds of sick, disappointed and angry men who had come home poor when they expected to be rich, and sick when they expected to be strong, had gone through the land, and folks began to think that Cathay was after all only a dream, and that the stories of great gold and of untold riches which they had heard were but "sailors' yarns" which no one could believe.

So it was hard to get together a crew large enough to man the six vessels that made up the fleet. At last, however, all was ready, and with a company of two hundred men, besides his sailors, Columbus hoisted anchor in the little port of San Lucar just north of Cadiz, near the mouth of the Guadalquivir river, and sailed away into the West.

This time he was determined to find the continent of Asia. Even though, as you remember, he made his men sign a paper saying that the coast of Cuba was Asia, he really seems to have doubted this himself. He felt that he had only found islands. If so, he said, Cathay must be the other side of those islands; and Cathay is what I must find.

So, with this plan in mind, he sent three of his ships to the little settlement of Isabella, and with the other three he sailed more to the southwest. On the first of August the ships came in sight of the three mountain peaks of the large island he called Trindad, or Trinity.

Look on your map of South America and you will see that Trinidad lies almost in the mouth of the Orinoco, a mighty river in the northern part of South America.

Columbus coasted about this island, and as he did so, looking across to the west, he saw what he supposed to be still another island. It was not. It was the coast of South America. For the first time, but without knowing it, Columbus saw the great continent he had so long been hunting for, though he had been seeking it under another name.

So you see, the story of Columbus shows how his life was full of mistakes. In his first voyage he found an island and thought it was the mainland of the Eastern Hemisphere; in his third voyage he discovered the mainland of the New World and thought it only an island off the coast of the Old World. His life was full of mistakes, but those mistakes have turned out to be, for us, glorious successes.

CHAPTER X. FROM PARADISE TO PRISON.

If you know a boy or a girl whose mind is set on any one thing, you will find that they are always talking about that thing. Is not this so? They have what people call a "hobby" (which is a kind of a horse, you know), and they are apt, as we say, to "ride their hobby to death."

If this is true of certain boys and girls, it is even more true of men and women. They get to be what we call people of one idea, and whatever they see or whatever they do always turns on that one idea.

It was so with Columbus. All his life his one idea had been the finding of Asia—the Indies, or Cathay, as he called it—by sailing to the west. He did sail to the west. He did find land. And, because of this, as we have seen, all his voyaging and all his exploring were done in the firm belief that he was discovering new parts of the eastern coast of Asia. The idea that he had found a new world never entered his head.

So, when he looked toward the west, as he sailed around the island of Trinidad and saw the distant shore, he said it was a new part of Asia. He was as certain of this as he had before been certain that Cuba was a part of the Asiatic mainland.

But when he sailed into the mouth of the great Orinoco River he was puzzled. For the water was no longer salt; it grew fresher and fresher as he sailed on. And it rushed out so furiously through the two straits at the northern and southern ends of Trinidad (which because of the terrible rush of their currents he called the Lion's Mouth and the Dragon's Mouth) that he was at first unable to explain it all.

Then he had a curious idea. Columbus was a great reader of the Bible; some of the Bible scholars of his day said that the Garden of Eden was in a far Eastern land where a mighty river came down through it from the hills of Paradise; as Columbus saw the beautiful land he had reached, and saw the great river sending down its waters to the sea, he fitted all that he saw to the Bible stories he knew so well, and felt sure that he had really discovered the entrance to the Garden of Eden.

He would gladly have sailed across the broad bay and up the great river to explore this heavenly land; but he was ill with gout, he was nearly blind from his sore eyes, his ships were shaky and leaky, and he felt that he ought to hurry away to the city of Isabella where his brothers, Bartholomew and Diego, were in charge of affairs and were, he knew, anxiously waiting for him to come back.

So at last he turned away from the lovely land that he thought must be Paradise and steered toward Hayti. On the nineteenth of August he arrived off the coast of Hayti. He sent a messenger with news of his arrival, and soon greeted his brother Bartholomew, who, when he heard of the Admiral's arrival, sailed at once to meet him.

Bartholomew Columbus had a sad story to tell his brother Christopher. Things had been going badly in Hayti, and the poor Admiral grew sicker and sicker as he listened to what Bartholomew had to tell.

You have heard it said that there are black sheep in every flock. There were black sheep in this colony of Columbus. There were lazy men and discontented men and jealous men, and they made great trouble, both in the city of Isabella and in the new town which Bartholomew bad built in another part of the island and called Santo Domingo.

Such men are sure to make mischief, and these men in Hayti had made a lot of it. Columbus had staid so long in Spain that these men began to say that they knew he was certainly in trouble or disgrace there, that the king and queen were angry with him, and that his offices of viceroy and admiral were to be taken away from him. If this were so, they were going to look out for themselves, they said. They would no longer obey the commands of the Admiral's brothers, Bartholomew and Diego, whom he had left in charge.

So they rose in rebellion, and made things so uncomfortable for the two brothers that the colony was soon full of strife and quarreling.

The leader of this revolt was one of the chief men in the colony. His name was Roldan. When Columbus and Bartholomew sailed into the harbor of Santo Domingo, on the thirtieth of August, they found that Roldan and his followers had set up a camp for themselves in another part of the island, and given out that they were determined never to have anything more to do with the three Columbus brothers.

This rebellion weakened the colony dreadfully. Things looked desperate; so desperate indeed that Columbus, after thinking it all over, thought that the only way to do was to seem to give in to Roldan and patch up some sort of an agreement by which they could all live together in peace. But all the same, he said, I will complain to the king and have this rebel Roldan punished.

So the Admiral wrote Roldan a letter in which he offered to forgive and forget all that he had done if he would come back and help make the colony strong and united again. Roldan agreed to do this, if he could have the same position he held before, and if Columbus would see that his followers had all the land they wanted. Columbus agreed to this and also gave the rebels permission to use the poor natives as slaves on their lands. So the trouble seemed to be over for a while, and Columbus sent two of his ships to Spain with letters to the king and queen. But in these letters he accused Roldan of rebellion and tried to explain why it was that things were going so badly in Hayti.

But when these ships arrived in Spain the tidings they brought and the other letters sent by them only made matters worse. People in Spain had heard so many queer things from across the sea that they were beginning to lose faith in Columbus. The men who had lost health and money in the unlucky second voyage of the Admiral were now lazy loafers about the docks, or they hung about the court and told how Columbus had made beggars of them, while they hooted after and insulted the two sons of Columbus who were pages in the queen's train. They called the boys the sons of "the Admiral of Mosquitoland."

Then came the ships with news of Roldan's rebellion, but with little or no gold. And people said this was a fine viceroy who couldn't keep order among his own men because, no doubt, he was too busy hiding away for his own use the gold and pearls they knew he must have found in the river of Paradise he said he had discovered.

Then came five shiploads of Indian slaves, sent to Spain by Columbus, and along with them came the story that Columbus had forgiven Roldan for his rebellion and given him lands and office in Hayti.

King Ferdinand had never really liked Columbus and had always been sorry that he had given him so much power and so large a share in the profits. The queen, too, began to think that while Columbus was a good sailor, he was a very poor governor. But when she heard of the shiploads of slaves he had sent, and found out that among the poor creatures were the daughters of some of the chiefs, or caciques, of the Indians, she was very angry, and asked how "her viceroy" dared to use "her vassals" so without letting her know about it. Things were indeed beginning to look bad for Columbus. The king and queen had promised that only members of the Admiral's family should be sent to govern the island; they had promised that no one but himself should have the right to trade in the new lands. But now they began to go back on their promises. If Columbus cannot find us gold and spices, they said, other men can. So they gave permission to other captains to explore and trade in the western lands. And as the complaints against the Admiral kept coming they began to talk of sending over some one else to govern the islands.

More letters came from Columbus asking the king and queen to let him keep up his slave-trade, and to send out some one to act as a judge of his quarrel with Roldan. Then the king and queen decided that something must be done at once. The queen ordered the return of the slaves Columbus had sent over, and the king told one of his officers named Bobadilla to go over to Hayti and set things straight. And he sent a letter by him commanding Columbus to talk with him, to give up all the forts and arms in the colony and to obey Bobadilla in all things.

Bobadilla sailed at once. But before he got across the sea matters, as we know, had been straightened out by the Admiral; and when Bobadilla reached Hayti he found everything quiet there. Columbus had made friends with Roldan (or made believe that he had), and had got things into good running order again.

This was not what Bobadilla had reckoned upon. He had expected to find things in such a bad way that he would have to take matters into his own hand at once, and become a greater man than the Admiral. If everything was all right he would have his journey for nothing and everybody would laugh at him. So he determined to go ahead, even though there was no necessity for his taking charge of affairs. He had been sent to do certain things, and he did them at once. Without asking Columbus for his advice or his assistance, he took possession of the forts and told every one that he was governor now. He said that he had come to set things straight, and he listened to the complaints of all the black sheep of the colony—and how they did crowd around him and say the worst things they could think of against the Admiral they had once been so anxious to follow.

Bobadilla listened to all their stories. He proceeded to use the power the king and queen had given him to punish and disgrace Columbus—which was not what they meant him to do. He moved into the palace of the Admiral; he ordered the Admiral and his brothers to come to him, and when they came expecting to talk things over, Bobadilla ordered that they be seized as prisoners and traitors, that they be chained hand and foot and put in prison.

Columbus's saddest day had come. The man who had found a new world for his king and queen, who had worked so hard in their service and who had meant to do right, although he had made many mistakes, was thrust into prison as if he were a thief or a murderer. The Admiral of the Ocean Seas, the Viceroy of the Indies, the grand man whom all Spain had honored and all the world had envied, was held as a prisoner in the land he had found, and all his powers were taken by a stranger. He was sick, he was disappointed, he was defeated in all his plans. And now he was in chains. His third voyage had ended the worst of all. He had sailed away to find Cathay; he had, so he believed, found the Garden of Eden and the river of Paradise. And here, as an end to it all, he was arrested by order of the king and queen he had tried to serve, his power and position were taken from him by an insolent and unpitying messenger from Spain; he was thrown into prison and after a few days he was hurried with his brothers on board a ship and sent to Spain for trial and punishment. How would it all turn out? Was it not a sad and sorry ending to his bright dreams of success?

CHAPTER XI. HOW THE ADMIRAL CAME AND WENT AGAIN.

I suppose you think Bobadilla was a very cruel man. He was. But in his time people were apt to be cruel to one another whenever they had the power in their own hands. The days in which Columbus lived were not like these in which we are living. You can never be too thankful for that, boys and girls. Bobadilla had been told to go over the water and set the Columbus matters straight. He had been brought up to believe that to set matters straight you must be harsh and cruel; and so he did as he was used to seeing other people in power do. Even Queen Isabella did not hesitate to do some dreadful things to certain people she did not like when she got them in her power. Cruelty was common in those days. It was what we call the "spirit of the age." So you must not blame Bobadilla too much, although we will all agree that it was very hard on Columbus.

So Columbus, as I have told you, sailed back to Spain. But when the officer who had charge of him and whose name was Villijo, had got out to sea and out of Bobadilla's sight, he wanted to take the chains off. For he loved Columbus and it made him feel very sad to see the old Admiral treated like a convict or a murderer. Let me have these cruel chains struck off, Your Excellency, he said. No, no, Villijo, Columbus replied. Let these fetters remain upon me. My king and queen ordered me to submit and Bobadilla has put me in chains. I will wear these irons until my king and queen shall order them removed, and I shall keep them always as relics and memorials of my services.

It always makes us sad to see any one in great trouble. To hear of a great man who has fallen low or of a rich man who has become poor, always makes us say: Is not that too bad? Columbus had many enemies in Spain. The nobles of the court, the men who had lost money in voyages to the Indies, the people whose fathers and sons and brothers had sailed away never to return, could not say anything bad enough about "this upstart Italian," as they called Columbus.

But to the most of the people Columbus was still the great Admiral. He was the man who had stuck to his one idea until he had made a friend of the queen; who had sailed away into the West and proved the Sea of Darkness and the Jumping-off place to be only fairy tales after all; who had found Cathay and the Indies for Spain. He was still a great man to the multitude.

So when on a certain October day, in the year 1500, it was spread abroad that a ship had just come into the harbor of Cadiz, bringing home the great Admiral, Christopher Columbus, a prisoner and in chains, folks began to talk at once. Why, who has done this? they cried. Is this the way to treat the man who found Cathay for Spain, the man whom the king and the queen delighted to honor, the man who made a procession for us with all sorts of birds and animals and pagan Indians? It cannot be. Why, we all remember how he sailed into Palos Harbor eight years ago and was received like a prince with banners and proclamations and salutes. And now to bring him home in chains! It is a shame; it is cruel; it is wicked. And when people began to talk in this way, the very ones who had said the worst things against him began to change their tone. As soon as the ship got into Cadiz, Columbus sent off a letter to a friend of his at the court in the beautiful city of Granada. This letter was, of course, shown to the queen. And it told all about what Columbus had suffered, and was, so full of sorrow and humbleness and yet of pride in what he had been able to do, even though he had been disgraced, that Queen Isabella (who was really a friend to Columbus in spite of her dissatisfaction with the things he sometimes did) became very angry at the way he had been treated.

She took the letter to King Ferdinand, and at once both the king and the queen hastened to send a messenger to Columbus telling him how angry and sorry they were that Bobadilla should have dared to treat their good friend the Admiral so. They ordered his immediate release from imprisonment; they sent him a present of five thousand dollars and asked him to come to court at once.

On the seventeenth of December, 1500, Columbus came to the court at Granada in the beautiful palace of the Alhambra. He rode on a mule. At that time, in Spain, people were not allowed to ride on mules, because if they did the Spanish horses would not be bought and sold, as mules were so much cheaper and were easier to ride. But Columbus was sick and it hurt him to ride horseback, while he could be fairly comfortable on an easy-going mule. So the king and queen gave him special permission to come on mule-back.

When Columbus appeared before the queen, looking so sick and troubled, Isabella was greatly affected. She thought of all he had done and all he had gone through and all he had suffered, and as he came to the steps of the throne the queen burst into tears. That made Columbus cry too, for he thought a great deal of the queen, and he fell at her feet and told her how much he honored her, and how much he was ready to do for her, if he could but have the chance.

Then the king and queen told him how sorry they were that any one should have so misunderstood their desires and have treated their brave and loyal Admiral so shamefully. They promised to make everything all right for him again, and to show him that they were his good friends now as they always had been since the day he first sailed away to find the Indies for them and for Spain.

Of course this made Columbus feel much better. He had left Hayti in fear and trembling. He had come home expecting something dreadful was going to happen; he would not have been surprised at a long imprisonment; he would not even have been surprised if he had been put to death—for the kings and queens and high lords of his day were very apt to order people put to death if they did not like what had been done. The harsh way in which Bobadilla had treated him made him think the king and queen had really ordered it. Perhaps they had; and perhaps the way in which the people cried out in indignation when they saw the great Admiral brought ashore in chains had its influence on Queen Isabella. King Ferdinand really cared nothing about it. He would gladly have seen Columbus put in prison for life; but the queen had very much to say about things in her kingdom, and so King Ferdinand made believe he was sorry and talked quite as pleasantly to Columbus as did the queen.

Now Columbus, as you must have found out by this time, was as quick to feel glad as he was to feel sad. And when he found that the king and queen were his friends once more, he became full of hope again and began to say where he would go and what he would do when he went back again as Viceroy of the Indies and Admiral of the Ocean Seas. He begged the queen to let him go back again at once, with ships and sailors and the power to do as he pleased in the islands he had found and in the lands he hoped to find.

They promised him everything, for promising is easy. But Columbus had once more to learn the truth of the old Bible warning that he had called to mind years before on the Bridge of Pinos: Put not your trust in princes.

The king and queen talked very nicely and promised much, but to one thing King Ferdinand had made up his mind—Columbus should never go back again to the Indies as viceroy or governor. And King Ferdinand was as stubborn as Columbus was persistent.

Not very much gold had yet been brought back from the Indies, but the king and queen knew from the reports of those who had been over the seas and kept their eyes open that, in time, a great deal of gold and treasure would come from there. So they felt that if they kept their promises to Columbus he would take away too large a slice of their profits, and if they let him have everything to say there it would not be possible to let other people, who were ready to share the profits with them, go off discovering on their own hook.

So they talked and delayed and sent out other expeditions and kept Columbus in Spain, unsatisfied. Another governor was sent over to take the place of Bobadilla, for they soon learned that that ungentlemanly knight was not even so good or so strict a governor as Columbus had been.

Almost two years passed in this way and still Columbus staid in Spain. At last the king and queen said he might go if he would not go near Hayti and would be sure to find other and better gold lands.

Columbus did not relish being told where to go and where not to go like this; but he promised. And on the ninth of May, 1502, with four small caravels and one hundred and fifty men, Christopher Columbus sailed from Cadiz on his fourth and last voyage to the western world.

He was now fifty-six years old. That is not an age at which we would call any one an old man. But Columbus had grown old long before his time. Care, excitement, exposure, peril, trouble and worry had made him white-haired and wrinkled. He was sick, he was nearly blind, he was weak, he was feeble—but his determination was just as firm, his hope just as high, his desire just as strong as ever. He was bound, this time, to find Cathay.

And he had one other wish. He had enemies in Hayti; they had laughed and hooted at him when he had been dragged off to prison and sent in chains on board the ship. He did wish to get even with them. He could not forgive them. He wanted to sail into the harbor of Isabella and Santo Domingo with his four ships and to say: See, all of you! Here I am again, as proud and powerful as ever. The king and queen have sent me over here once more with ships and sailors at my command. I am still the Admiral of the Ocean Seas and all you tried to do against me has amounted to nothing.

This is not the right sort of a spirit to have, either for men or boys; it is not wise or well to have it gratified. Forgiveness is better than vengeance; kindliness is better than pride.

At any rate, it was not to be gratified with Columbus. When his ships arrived off the coast of Hayti, although his orders from the king and queen were not to stop at the island going over, the temptation to show himself was too strong. He could not resist it. So he sent word to the new governor, whose name was Ovando, that he had arrived with his fleet for the discovery of new lands in the Indies, and that he wished to come into Santo Domingo Harbor as one of his ships needed repairs; he would take the opportunity, he said, of mending his vessel and visiting the governor at the same time.

Now it so happened that Governor Ovando was just about sending to Spain a large fleet. And in these ships were to go some of the men who had treated Columbus so badly. Bobadilla, the ex-governor, was one of them; so was the rebel Roldan who had done so much mischief; and there were others among the passengers and prisoners whom Columbus disliked or who hated Columbus. There was also to go in the fleet a wonderful cargo of gold—the largest amount yet sent across to Spain. There were twenty-six ships in all, in the great gold fleet, and the little city of Santo Domingo was filled with excitement and confusion.

We cannot altogether make out whether Governor Ovando was a friend to Columbus or not. At any rate, he felt that it would be unwise and unsafe for Columbus to come into the harbor or show himself in the town when so many of his bitter enemies were there. So he sent back word to Columbus that he was sorry, but that really he could not let him come in.

How bad that must have made the old Admiral feel! To be refused admission to the place he had found and built up for Spain! It was unkind, he said; he must and would go in.

Just then Columbus, who was a skillful sailor and knew all the signs of the sky, and all about the weather, happened to notice the singular appearance of the sky, and saw that there was every sign that a big storm was coming on. So he sent word to Governor Ovando again, telling him of this, and asking permission to run into the harbor of Santo Domingo with his ships to escape the coming storm. But the governor could not see that any storm was coming on. He said: Oh! that is only another way for the Admiral to try to get around me and get me to let him in. I can't do it. So, he sent back word a second time that he really could not, let Columbus come in. I know you are a very clever sailor, he said, but, really, I think you must be mistaken about this storm. At any rate, you will have time to go somewhere else before it comes on, and I shall be much obliged if you will.

Now, among the twenty-six vessels of the gold fleet was one in which was stored some of the gold that belonged to Columbus as his share, according to his arrangement with the king and queen. If a storm came on, this vessel would be in danger, to say nothing of all the rest of the fleet. So Columbus sent in to Governor Ovando a third time. He told him he was certain a great storm was coming. And he begged the governor, even if he was not allowed to come up to Santo Domingo, by all means to keep the fleet in the harbor until the storm was over. If you don't, there will surely be trouble, he said. And then he sailed with his ships along shore looking for a safe harbor.

But the people in Santo Domingo put no faith in the Admiral's "probabilities." There will be no storm, the captains and the officers said. If there should be our ships are strong enough to stand it. The Admiral Columbus is getting to be timid as he grows older. And in spite of the old sailor's warning, the big gold fleet sailed out of the harbor of Santo Domingo and headed for Spain.

But almost before they had reached the eastern end of the island of Hayti, the storm that Columbus had prophesied burst upon them.

It was a terrible tempest. Twenty of the ships went to the bottom. The great gold fleet was destroyed. The enemies of Columbus—Bobadilla, Roldan and the rest were drowned. Only a few of the ships managed to get back into Santo Domingo Harbor, broken and shattered. And the only ship of all the great fleet that got safely through the storm and reached Spain all right was the one that carried on board the gold that belonged to Columbus. Was not that singular?

Then all the friends of Columbus cried: How wonderful! Truly the Lord is on the side of the great Admiral!

But his enemies said: This Genoese is a wizard. He was mad because the governor would not let him come into the harbor, and he raised this storm in revenge. It is a dangerous thing to interfere with the Admiral's wishes.

For you see in those days people believed in witches and spells and all kinds of fairy-book things like those, when they could not explain why things happened. And when they could not give a good reason for some great disaster or for some stroke of bad luck, they just said: It is witchcraft; and left it so.

CHAPTER XII. HOW THE ADMIRAL PLAYED ROBINSON CRUSOE.

While the terrible storm that wrecked the great gold fleet of the governor was raging so furiously, Columbus with his four ships was lying as near shore as he dared in a little bay farther down the coast of Hayti. Here he escaped the full fury of the gale, but still his ships suffered greatly, and came very near being shipwrecked. They became separated in the storm, but the caravels met at last after the storm was over and steered away for the island of Jamaica.

For several days they sailed about among the West India Islands; then they took a westerly course, and on the thirtieth of July, Columbus saw before him the misty outlines of certain high mountains which he supposed to be somewhere in Asia, but which we now know were the Coast Range Mountains of Honduras. And Honduras, you remember, is a part of Central America. Just turn to the map of Central America in your geography and find Honduras. The mountains, you see, are marked there; and on the northern coast, at the head of a fine bay, you will notice the seaport town of Truxillo. And that is about the spot where, for the first time, Columbus saw the mainland of North America.

As he sailed toward the coast a great canoe came close to the ship. It was almost as large as one of his own caravels, for it was over forty feet long and fully eight feet wide. It was paddled by twenty-five Indians, while in the middle, under an awning of palm-thatch sat the chief Indian, or cacique, as he was called. A curious kind of sail had been rigged to catch the breeze, and the canoe was loaded with fruits and Indian merchandise.

This canoe surprised Columbus very much. He had seen nothing just like it among the other Indians he had visited. The cacique and his people, too, were dressed in clothes and had sharp swords and spears. He thought of the great galleys of Venice and Genoa; he remembered the stories that had come to him of the people of Cathay; he believed that, at last, he had come to the right place. The shores ahead of him were, he was sure, the coasts of the Cathay he was hunting for, and these people in "the galley of the cacique" were much nearer the kind of people he was expecting to meet than were the poor naked Indians of Hayti and Cuba.

In a certain way he was right. These people in the big canoe were, probably, some of the trading Indians of Yucatan, and beyond them, in what we know to-day as Mexico, was a race of Indians, known as Aztecs, who were what is called half-civilized; for they had cities and temples and stone houses and almost as much gold and treasure as Columbus hoped to find in his fairyland of Cathay. But Columbus was not to find Mexico. Another daring and cruel Spanish captain, named Cortez, discovered the land, conquered it for Spain, stripped it of its gold and treasure, and killed or enslaved its brave and intelligent people.

After meeting this canoe, Columbus steered for the distant shore. He coasted up and down looking for a good harbor, and on the seventeenth of August, 1502, he landed as has been told you, near what is now the town of Truxillo, in Honduras. There, setting up the banner of Castile, he took possession of the country in the name of the king and queen of Spain.

For the first time in his life Columbus stood on the real soil of the New World. All the islands he had before discovered and colonized were but outlying pieces of America. Now he was really upon the American Continent.

But he did not know it. To him it was but a part of Asia. And as the main purpose of this fourth voyage was to find a way to sail straight to India—which he supposed lay somewhere to the south—he set off on his search. The Indians told him of "a narrow place" that he could find by sailing farther south, and of a "great water." beyond it. This "narrow place" was the Isthmus of Panama, and the "great water" beyond it was, of course, the Pacific Ocean. But Columbus thought that by a "narrow place" they meant a strait instead of an isthmus. If he could but find that strait, he could sail through it into the great Bay of Bengal which, as you know and as he had heard, washes the eastern shore of India.

So he sailed along the coasts of Honduras and Nicaragua trying to find the strait he was hunting for. Just look at your map and see how near he was to the way across to the Pacific that men are now digging out, and which, as the Nicaragua Canal, will connect the Atlantic and the Pacific Oceans. And think how near he was to finding that Pacific Ocean over which, if he could but have got across the Isthmus of Panama, he could have sailed to the Cathay and the Indies he spent his life in trying to find. But if he had been fortunate enough to get into the waters of the Pacific, I do not believe it would have been so lucky for him, after all. His little ships, poorly built and poorly provisioned, could never have sailed that great ocean in safety, and the end might have proved even more disastrous than did the Atlantic voyages of the Admiral.

He soon understood that he had found a richer land than the islands he had thus far discovered. Gold and pearls were much more plentiful along the Honduras coast than they were in Cuba and Hayti, and Columbus decided that, after he had found India, he would come back by this route and collect a cargo of the glittering treasures.

The land was called by the Indians something that sounded very much like Veragua. This was the name Columbus gave to it; and it was this name, Veragua, that was afterward given to the family of Columbus as its title; so that, to-day, the living descendant of Christopher Columbus in Spain is called the Duke of Veragua.

But as Columbus sailed south, along what is called "the Mosquito Coast," the weather grew stormy and the gales were severe. His ships were crazy and worm-eaten; the food was running low; the sailors began to grumble and complain and to say that if they kept on in this way they would surely starve before they could reach India.

Columbus, too, began to grow uneasy. His youngest son, Ferdinand, a brave, bright little fellow of thirteen, had come with him on this voyage, and Columbus really began to be afraid that something might happen to the boy, especially if the crazy ships should be wrecked, or if want of food should make them all go hungry. So at last he decided to give up hunting for the strait that should lead him into the Bay of Bengal; he felt obliged, also, to give up his plan of going back to the Honduras coast for gold and pearls. He turned his ships about and headed for Hayti where he hoped he could get Governor Ovando to give him better ships so that he could try it all over again.

Here, you see, was still another disappointing defeat for Columbus. For after he had been on the American coast for almost a year; after he had come so near to what he felt to be the long-looked-for path to the Indies; after most wonderful adventures on sea and land, he turned his back on it all, without really having accomplished what he set out to do and, as I have told you, steered for Hayti.

But it was not at all easy to get to Hayti in those leaky ships of his. In fact it was not possible to get there with them at all; for on the twenty-third of June, 1503, when he had reached the island of Jamaica he felt that his ships would not hold out any longer. They were full of worm-holes; they were leaking badly; they were strained and battered from the storms. He determined, therefore, to find a good harbor somewhere on the island of Jamaica and go in there for repairs. But he could not find a good one; his ships grew worse and worse; every day's delay was dangerous; and for fear the ships would sink and carry the crews to the bottom of the sea, Columbus decided to run them ashore anyhow. This he did; and on the twelfth of August, 1503, he deliberately headed for the shore and ran his ships aground in a little bay on the island of Jamaica still known as Sir Christopher's Cove. And there the fleet was wrecked.

The castaways lashed the four wrecks together; they built deck-houses and protections so as to make themselves as comfortable as possible, and for a whole year Columbus and his men lived there at Sir Christopher's Cove on the beautiful island of Jamaica.

It proved anything but beautiful for them, however. It makes a good deal of difference, you know, in enjoying things whether you are well and happy. If you are hungry and can't get anything to eat, the sky does not look so blue or the trees so green as if you were sitting beneath them with a jolly picnic party and with plenty of lunch in the baskets.

It was no picnic for Columbus and his companions. That year on the island of Jamaica was one of horror, of peril, of sickness, of starvation. Twice, a brave comrade named Diego Mendez started in an open boat for Hayti to bring relief. The first time he was nearly shipwrecked, but the second time he got away all right. And then for months nothing was heard of him, and it was supposed that he had been drowned. But the truth was that Governor Ovando, had an idea that the king and queen of Spain were tired of Columbus and would not feel very bad if they never saw him again. He promised to send help, but did not do so for fear he should get into trouble. And the relief that the poor shipwrecked people on Jamaica longed for did not come.

Then some of the men who were with Columbus mutinied and ran away. In fact, more things happened during this remarkable fourth voyage of Columbus than I can begin to tell you about. The story is more wonderful than is that of Robinson Crusoe, and when you are older you must certainly read it all and see just what marvelous adventures Columbus and his men met with and how bravely the little Ferdinand Columbus went through them all. For when Ferdinand grew up he wrote a life of his father, the Admiral, and told the story of how they all played Robinson Crusoe at Sir Christopher's Cove.

At last the long-delayed help was sent by Governor Ovando, and one day the brave Diego Mendez came sailing into Sir Christopher's Cove. And Columbus forgave the rebels who had run away; and on the twenty-eighth of June, 1504, they all sailed away from the place, that, for a year past, had been almost worse than a prison to them all.

On the fifteenth of August, the rescued crews sailed into the harbor of Santo Domingo. The governor, Ovando, who had reluctantly agreed to send for Columbus, was now in a hurry to get him away. Whether the governor was afraid of him, or ashamed because of the way he had treated him, or whether he felt that Columbus was no longer held so high in Spain, and that, therefore, it was not wise to make much of him, I cannot say. At any rate he hurried him off to Spain, and on the twelfth of September, 1504, Columbus turned his back forever on the new world he had discovered, and with two ships sailed for Spain.

He had not been at sea but a day or two before he found that the ship in which he and the boy Ferdinand were sailing was not good for much. A sudden storm carried away its mast and the vessel was sent back to Santo Domingo. Columbus and Ferdinand, with a few of the men, went on board the other ship which was commanded by Bartholomew Columbus, the brother of the Admiral, who had been with him all through the dreadful expedition. At last they saw the home shores again, and on the seventh of November, 1504, Columbus sailed into the harbor of San Lucar, not far from Cadiz.

He had been away from Spain for fully two years and a half. He had not accomplished a single thing he set out to do. He had met with disappointment and disaster over and over again, and had left the four ships that had been given him a total wreck upon the shores of Jamaica. He came back poor, unsuccessful, unnoticed, and so ill that he could scarcely get ashore.

And so the fourth voyage of the great Admiral ended. It was his last. His long sickness had almost made him crazy. He said and did many odd things, such as make us think, nowadays, that people have, as we call it, "lost their minds." But he was certain of one thing—the king and queen of Spain had not kept the promises they had made him, and he was determined, if he lived, to have justice done him, and to make them do as they said they would.

They had told him that only himself or one of his family should be Admiral of the Ocean Seas and Viceroy of the New Lands; they had sent across the water others, who were not of his family, to govern what he had been promised for his own. They had told him that he should have a certain share of the profits that came from trading and gold hunting in the Indies; they had not

kept this promise either, and he was poor when he was certain he ought to be rich.
So, when he was on land once more, he tried hard to get to court and see the king and queen. But he was too sick.
He had got as far as beautiful Seville, the fair Spanish city by the Guadalquivir, and there he had to give up and go to, bed. And then came a new disappointment. He was to lose his best friend at the court. For when he had been scarcely two weeks in Spain, Queen Isabella died.
She was not what would be considered in these days either a particularly good woman, or an especially good queen. She did many cruel things; and while she talked much about doing good, she was generally looking out for herself most of all. But that was not so much her fault as the fault of the times in which she lived. Her life was not a happy one; but she had always felt kindly toward Columbus, and when he was where he could see her and talk to her, he had always been able to get her to side with him and grant his wishes.
Columbus was now a very sick man. He had to keep his bed most of the time, and this news of the queen's death made him still worse, for he felt that now no one who had the "say" would speak a good word for the man who had done so much for Spain, and given to the king and queen the chance to make their nation great and rich and powerful.

CHAPTER XIII. THE END OF THE STORY.

Any one who is sick, as some of you may know, is apt to be anxious and fretful and full of fears as to how he is going to get along, or who will look out for his family. Very often there is no need for this feeling; very often it is a part of the complaint from which the sick person is suffering.
In the case of Columbus, however, there was good cause for this depressed and anxious feeling. King Ferdinand, after Queen Isabella's death, did nothing to help Columbus. He would not agree to give the Admiral what he called his rights, and though Columbus kept writing letters from his sick room asking for justice, the king would do nothing for him. And when the king's smile is turned to a frown, the fashion of the court is to frown, too.
So Columbus had no friends at the king's court. Diego, his eldest son, was still one of the royal pages, but he could do nothing. Without friends, without influence, without opportunity, Columbus began to feel that he should never get his rights unless he could see the king himself. And sick though he was he determined to try it.
It must have been sad enough to see this sick old man drag himself feebly to the court to ask for justice from the king whom he had enriched. You would think that when King Ferdinand really saw Columbus at the foot of the throne, and when he remembered all that this man had done for him and for Spain, and how brave and persistent and full of determination to do great things the Admiral once had been, he would at least have given the old man what was justly due him.
But he would not. He smiled on the old sailor, and said many pleasant things and talked as if he were a friend, but he would not agree to anything Columbus asked him; and the poor Admiral crawled back to his sick bed again, and gave up the struggle. I have done all that I can do, he said to the few friends who remained faithful to him; I must leave it all to God. He has always helped me when things were at the worst.
And God helped him by taking him away from all the fret, and worry, and pain, and struggle that made up so much of the Admiral's troubled life. On the twentieth of May, 1506, the end came. In the house now known as Number 7 Columbus Avenue, in the city of Valladolid; in Northern

Spain, with a few faithful friends at his side, he signed his will, lay back in bed and saying trustfully these words: Into thy hands, O Lord, I commit my spirit! the Admiral of the Ocean Seas, the Viceroy of the Indies, the Discoverer of a New World, ended his fight for life. Christopher Columbus was dead.

He was but sixty years old. With Tennyson, and Whittier, and Gladstone, and De Lesseps living to be over eighty, and with your own good grandfather and grandmother, though even older than Columbus, by no means ready to be called old people, sixty years seems an early age to be so completely broken and bent and gray as was he. But trouble, and care, and exposure, and all the worries and perils of his life of adventure, had, as you must know, so worn upon Columbus that when he died he seemed to be an old, old man. He was white-haired, you remember, even before he discovered America, and each year he seemed to grow older and grayer and more feeble.

And after he had died in that lonely house in Valladolid, the world seems for a time to have almost forgotten him. A few friends followed him to the grave; the king, for whom he had done so much, did not trouble himself to take any notice of the death of his Admiral, whom once he had been forced to honor, receive and reward. The city of Valladolid, in which Columbus died, was one of those fussy little towns in which everybody knew what was happening next door, and talked and argued about whatever happened upon its streets and in its homes; and yet even Valladolid hardly seemed to know of the presence within its gates of the sick "Viceroy of the Indies." Not until four weeks after his death did the Valladolid people seem to realize what had happened; and then all they did was to write down this brief record: "The said Admiral is dead."

To-day, the bones of Columbus inclosed in a leaden casket lie in the Cathedral of Santo Domingo. People have disputed about the place where the Discoverer of America was born; they are disputing about the place where he is buried. But as it seems now certain that he was born in Genoa, so it seems also certain that his bones are really in the tomb in the old Cathedral at Santo Domingo, that old Haytian city which he founded, and where he had so hard a time.

At least a dozen places in the Old World and the New have built monuments and statues in his honor; in the United States, alone, over sixty towns and villages bear his name, or the kindred one of Columbia. The whole world honors him as the Discoverer of America; and yet the very name that the Western Hemisphere bears comes not from the man who discovered it, but from his friend and comrade Americus Vespucius.

Like Columbus, this Americus Vespucius was an Italian; like him, he was a daring sailor and a fearless adventurer, sailing into strange seas to see what he could find. He saw more of the American coast than did Columbus, and not being so full of the gold-hunting and slave-getting fever as was the Admiral, he brought back from his four voyages so much information about the new-found lands across the sea, that scholars, who cared more for news than gold, became interested in what he reported. And some of the map-makers in France, when they had to name the new lands in the West that they drew on their maps—the lands that were not the Indies, nor China, nor Japan—called them after the man who had told them so much about them—Americus Vespucius. And so it is that to-day you live in America and not in Columbia, as so many people have thought this western world of ours should be named.

And even the titles, and riches, and honors that the king and queen of Spain promised to Columbus came very near being lost by his family, as they had been by himself. It was only by the hardest work, and by keeping right at it all the time, that the Admiral's eldest son, Diego Columbus, almost squeezed out of King Ferdinand of Spain the things that had been promised to his father.

But Diego was as plucky, and as brave, and as persistent as his father had been; then, too, he had lived at court so long—he was one of the queen's pages, you remember that he knew just what to do and how to act so as to get what he wanted. And at last he got it.

He was made Viceroy over the Indies; he went across the seas to Hayti, and in his palace in the city of Santo Domingo he ruled the lands his father had found, and which for centuries were known as the Spanish Main; he was called Don Diego; he married a high-born lady of Spain, the niece of King Ferdinand; he received the large share of "the riches of the Indies" that his father had worked for, but never received. And the family of Christopher Columbus, the Genoese adventurer—under the title of the Dukes of Veragua—have, ever since Don Diego's day, been of what is called "the best blood of Spain."

If you have read this story of Christopher Columbus aright, you must have come to the conclusion that the life of this Italian sea captain who discovered a new world was not a happy one. From first to last it was full of disappointment. Only once, in all his life, did he know what happiness and success meant, and that was on his return from his first voyage, when he landed amid cheers of welcome at Palos, and marched into Barcelona in procession like a conqueror to be received as an equal by his king and queen.

Except for that little taste of glory, how full of trouble was his life! He set out to find Cathay and bring back its riches and its treasures. He did not get within five thousand miles of Cathay. He returned from his second voyage a penitent, bringing only tidings of disaster. He returned from his third voyage in disgrace, a prisoner and in chains, smarting under false charges of theft, cruelty and treason. He returned from his fourth voyage sick unto death, unnoticed, unhonored, unwelcomed.

From first to last he was misunderstood. His ideas were made fun of, his efforts were treated with contempt, and even what he did was not believed, or was spoken of as of not much account. A career that began in scorn ended in neglect. He died unregarded, and for years no one gave him credit for what he had done, nor honor for what he had brought about.

Such a life would, I am sure, seem to all boys and girls, but a dreary prospect if they felt it was to be theirs or that of any one they loved. And yet what man to-day is more highly honored than Christopher Columbus? People forget all the trials and hardships and sorrows of his life, and think of him only as one of the great successes of the world—the man who discovered America. And out of his life of disaster and disappointment two things stand forth that all of us can honor and all of us should wish to copy. These are his sublime persistence and his unfaltering faith.

Even as a boy, Columbus had an idea of what he wished to try and what he was bound to do. He kept right at that idea, no matter what might happen to annoy him or set him back.

It was the faith and the persistence of Columbus that discovered America and opened the way for the millions who now call it their home. It is because of these qualities that we honor him to-day; it is because this faith and persistence ended as they did in the discovery of a new world, that to-day his fame is immortal.

Other men were as brave, as skillful and as wise as he. Following in his track they came sailing to the new lands; they explored its coasts, conquered its red inhabitants, and peopled its shores with the life that has made America today the home of millions of white men and millions of free men. But Columbus showed the way.

CHAPTER XIV. HOW THE STORY TURNS OUT.

Whenever you start to read a story that you hope will be interesting, you always wonder, do you not, how it is going to turn out? Your favorite fairy tale or wonder story that began with "once upon a time," ends, does it not, "so the prince married the beautiful princess, and they lived happy ever after?"

Now, how does this story that we have been reading together turn out? You don't think it ended happily, do you? It was, in some respects, more marvelous than any fairy tale or wonder story; but, dear me! you say, why couldn't Columbus have lived happily, after he had gone through so much, and done so much, and discovered America, and given us who came after him so splendid a land to live in?

Now, just here comes the real point of the story. Wise men tell us that millions upon millions of busy little insects die to make the beautiful coral islands of the Southern seas. Millions and millions of men and women have lived and labored, died and been forgotten by the world they helped to make the bright, and beautiful, and prosperous place to live in that it is to-day. Columbus was one of these millions; but he was a leader among them and has not been forgotten. As the world has got farther away from the time in which he lived, the man Columbus, who did so much and yet died almost unnoticed, has grown more and more famous; his name is immortal, and to-day he is the hero Columbus—one of the world's greatest men.

We, in America, are fond of celebrating anniversaries. I suppose the years that you boys and girls have thus far lived have been the most remarkable in the history of the world for celebrating anniversaries. For fully twenty years the United States has been keeping its birthday. The celebration commenced long before you were born, with the one hundredth anniversary of the Battle of Lexington (in 1875). It has not ended yet. But in 1892, We celebrated the greatest of all our birthdays—the discovery of the continent that made it possible for us to be here at all.

Now this has not always been so with us. I suppose that in 1592 and in 1692 no notice whatever was taken of the twelfth day of October, on which—one hundred and two hundred years before—Columbus had landed on that flat little "key" known as Watling's Island down among the West Indies, and had begun a new chapter in the world's wonderful story. In 1592, there was hardly anybody here to celebrate the anniversary—in fact, there was hardly anybody here at all, except a few Spanish settlers in the West Indies, in Mexico, and in Florida. In 1692, there were a few scattered settlements of Frenchmen in Canada, of Englishmen in New England, Dutchmen in New York, Swedes in Delaware, and Englishmen in Maryland, Virginia and the Carolinas. But none of these people loved the Spaniards. They hated them, indeed; for there had been fierce fighting going on for nearly a hundred years between Spain and England, and you couldn't find an Englishman, a Dutchman or a Swede who was willing to say a good word for Spain, or thank God for the man who sailed away in Spanish ships to discover America two hundred years before.

In 1792, people did think a little more about this, and there were a few who did remember that, three hundred years before, Columbus had found the great continent upon which, in that year 1792, a new republic, called the United States of America, had only just been started after a long and bloody war of rebellion and revolution.

We do not find, however, that in that year of 1792 there were many, if any, public celebrations of the Discovery of America, in America itself. A certain American clergyman, however, whose name was the Rev. Elhanan Winchester, celebrated the three hundredth anniversary of the Discovery of America by Columbus. And he celebrated it not in America, but in England, where he was then living. On the twelfth of October, 1792, Winchester delivered an address on "Columbus and his Discoveries," before a great assembly of interested listeners. In that address he said some very enthusiastic and some very remarkable things about the America that was to be:

"I see the United States rise in all their ripened glory before me," he said. "I look through and beyond every yet peopled region of the New World, and behold period still brightening upon period. Where one contiguous depth of gloomy wilderness now shuts out even the beams of day, I see new States and empires, new seats of wisdom and knowledge, new religious domes spreading around. In places now untrod by any but savage beasts, or men as savage as they, I hear the voices of happy labor, and see beautiful cities rising to view. I behold the whole continent highly cultivated and fertilized, full of cities, towns and villages, beautiful and lovely beyond expression. I hear the praises of my great Creator sung upon the banks of those rivers now unknown to song. Behold the delightful prospect! See the silver and gold of America employed in the service of the Lord of the whole earth! See slavery, with all its train of attendant evils, forever abolished! See a communication opened through the whole continent, from North to South and from East to West, through a most fruitful country. Behold the glory of God extending, and the gospel spreading through the whole land!"

Of course, it was easy for a man to see and to hope and to say all this; but it is a little curious, is it not, that he should have seen things just as they have turned out?

In Mr. Winchester's day, the United States of America had not quite four millions of inhabitants. In his day Virginia was the largest State—in the matter of population—Pennsylvania was the second and New York the third. Philadelphia was the greatest city, then followed New York, Boston, Baltimore and Charleston. Chicago was not even thought of.

To-day, four hundred years after Columbus first saw American shores, one hundred and sixteen years after the United States were started in life by the Declaration of American Independence, these same struggling States of one hundred years ago are joined together to make the greatest and most prosperous nation in the world. With a population of more than sixty-two millions of people; with the thirteen original States grown into forty-four, with the population of its three largest cities—New York; Philadelphia and Chicago—more than equal to the population of the whole country one hundred years ago; with schools and colleges and happy homes brightening the whole broad land that now stretches from ocean to ocean, the United States leads all other countries in the vast continent Columbus discovered. Still westward, as Columbus led, the nation advances; and, in a great city that Columbus could never have imagined, and that the prophet of one hundred years ago scarcely dreamed of, the mighty Republic in 1892 invited all the rest of the world to join with it in celebrating the four hundredth anniversary of the Discovery of America by Columbus the Admiral. And to do this celebrating fittingly and grandly, it built up the splendid White City by the great Fresh Water Sea.

Columbus was a dreamer; he saw such wonderful visions of what was to be, that people, as we know, tapped their foreheads and called him "the crazy Genoese." But not even the wildest fancies nor the most wonderful dreams of Columbus came anywhere near to what he would really have seen if—he could have visited the Exposition at Chicago, in the great White City by the lake—a "show city" specially built for the World's Fair of 1893, given in his honor and as a monument to his memory.

Why, he would say, the Cathay that I spent my life trying to find was but a hovel alongside this! What would he have seen? A city stretching a mile and a half in length, and more than half a mile in breadth; a space covering over five hundred acres of ground, and containing seventeen magnificent buildings, into any one of which could have been put the palaces of all the kings and queens of Europe known to Columbus's day. And in these buildings he would have seen gathered together, all the marvelous and all the useful things, all the beautiful and all the delightful things that the world can make to-day, arranged and displayed for all the world to see. He would have stood amazed in that wonderful city of glass and iron, that surpassingly beautiful city, all of purest white, that had been built some eight miles from the center of big and busy Chicago, looking out upon the blue waters of mighty Lake Michigan. It was a city that I wish all the boys and girls of America—especially all who read this story of the man in whose honor it was built, might have visited. For as they saw all its wonderful sights, studied its marvelous exhibits, and enjoyed its beautiful belongings, they would have been ready to say how proud, and glad, and happy they were to think that they were American girls and boys, living in this wonderful nineteenth century that has been more crowded with marvels, and mysteries, and triumphs than any one of the Arabian Nights ever contained.

But, whether you saw the Columbian Exhibition or not, you can say that. And then stop and think what a parrot did. That is one of the most singular things in all this wonder story you are reading. Do you not remember how, when Columbus was slowly feeling his way westward, Captain Alonso Pinzon saw some parrots flying southward, and believing from this that the land they sought was off in that direction, he induced Columbus to change his course from the west to the south? If Columbus had not changed his course and followed the parrots, the Santa Maria, with the Pinta and the Nina, would have sailed on until they had entered the harbor of Savannah or Charleston, or perhaps the broad waters of Chesapeake Bay. Then the United States of to-day would have been discovered and settled by Spaniards, and the whole history of the land would have been quite different from what it has been. Spanish blood has peopled, but not uplifted, the countries of South America and the Spanish Main. English blood, which, following after—because Columbus had first shown the way—peopled, saved and upbuilt the whole magnificent northern land that Spain missed and lost. They have found in it more gold than ever Columbus dreamed of in his never-found Cathay; they have filled it with a nobler, braver, mightier, and more numerous people than ever Columbus imagined the whole mysterious land of the Indies contained; they have made it the home of freedom, of peace, of education, of intelligence and of progress, and have protected and bettered it until the whole world respects it for its strength, honors it for its patriotism, admires it for its energy, and marvels at it for its prosperity.

And this is what a flying parrot did: It turned the tide of lawless adventure, of gold-hunting, of slave-driving, and of selfish strife for gain to the south; it left the north yet unvisited until it was ready for the strong, and sturdy, and determined men and women who, hunting for liberty, came across the seas and founded the colonies that became in time the free and independent republic of the United States of America.

And thus has the story of Columbus really turned out. Happier than any fairy tale, more marvelous than any wonder book, the story of the United States of America is one that begins, "Once upon a time," and has come to the point where it depends upon the boys and girls who read it, to say whether or not they shall "live happily ever after."

The four hundred years of the New World's life closed its chapter of happiness in the electric lights and brilliant sunshine of the marvelous White City by Lake Michigan. It is a continued story of daring, devotion and progress, that the boys and girls of America should never tire of reading. And this story was made possible and turned out so well, because of the briefer, but no less interesting story of the daring, the devotion and the faith of the determined Genoese sailor of four hundred years ago, whom men knew as Don Christopher Columbus, the Admiral of the Ocean Seas.

Made in the USA
Middletown, DE
03 November 2015